Power in the 21st Century

Power in the 21st Century

Conversations with John A. Hall

Michael Mann

polity

Copyright © Michael Mann and John A. Hall 2011

The right of Michael Mann and John A. Hall to be identified as
Authors of this Work has been asserted in accordance with the UK
Copyright, Designs and Patents Act 1988.

First published in 2011 by Polity Press

Polity Press
65 Bridge Street
Cambridge CB2 1UR, UK

Polity Press
350 Main Street
Malden, MA 02148, USA

ISBN-13: 978-0-7456-5322-8
ISBN-13: 978-0-7456-5323-5(pb)

A catalogue record for this book is available from the British Library.

Typeset in 11 on 13 pt Sabon
by Toppan Best-set Premedia Limited
Printed and bound in Great Britain by MPG Books Group Limited,
Bodmin, Cornwall

The publisher has used its best endeavors to ensure that the URLs for
external websites referred to in this book are correct and active at the
time of going to press. However, the publisher has no responsibility for
the websites and can make no guarantee that a site will remain live or
that the content is or will remain appropriate.

Every effort has been made to trace all copyright holders, but if any
have been inadvertently overlooked the publisher will be pleased to
include any necessary credits in any subsequent reprint or edition.

For further information on Polity, visit our website:
www.politybooks.com

Contents

Introduction (John A. Hall)   1

Part One: Powers in Motion   9

Chapter One: Capitalism   11

Chapter Two: Militarism   27

Chapter Three: Political Power   41

Chapter Four: An End to Ideology?   64

Chapter Five: Patterns, Cages, Interstices,
               and a Dialectic   70

Part Two: The Nature of Social Change   79

Chapter Six: States, Strong and Weak   81

Chapter Seven: Group Agency   107

Chapter Eight: Outcomes   119

Chapter Nine: Contingencies of Modernity   132

Chapter Ten: Our Looming Crisis   151

Conclusion   169

References   177

Introduction

John A. Hall

Michael Mann has always seemed to me to be "our" generation's Max Weber.[1] The most obvious way in which this is
so is that of his central theoretical claim: namely, that it is
necessary to take into account distinct sources of social
power in order to understand both the historical record and
the contours of our own world. Just as important is the
fantastic historical range of both thinkers, allied to stagger-
ing abilities to absorb and condense huge amounts of empirical evidence. Of course, there are subtle differences, some of
which Mann remarks upon late in the following text. Weber's
concern with economic, political, and ideological forms of
power is developed by Mann into a fourfold scheme that
adds to the celebrated trinity an insistence on the autonomy
of military power. Then there is a difference in perspective.
The extended scholarship that Weber devoted to different
civilizations is not fully matched by Mann, despite striking
forays made in that direction. But the most crucial difference
is normative. It is impossible to overstate the influence of

[1] The claim is made at some length in my "Political Questions."
Please note that this and all other texts or authors mentioned in
the conversations that follow are fully cited at the end of this
volume.

Nietzsche on Weber, leading as it did to his concern with disenchantment—and at times to a politics that had little time for liberal democracy, favoring as it did nationalism together with the need for a charismatic leader to shake society out of the malaise of consumerist dullness. In contrast, Mann is a committed social democrat, as this volume makes clearer than ever before. This reinforces the sense that he is indeed a Max Weber for our times. He is as concerned with our current sense of history, but grounds his work in values that are closer to our own.

Though Mann's work is very well known, it may be useful to recall something of the grandeur of his attempt at social understanding. He has told us that he began his attempt to develop the tools to understand the historical record as a whole in 1972, imagining at that time that he could manage this in short order and within a single volume. He was incapable of doing this, to our very great benefit! We have instead been offered large books crammed with detail on key turning points, all of them concerned both to advance sociological theory and to help social understanding.

The Sources of Social Power, Volume One: A History of Power from the Beginning to 1760 AD is a particularly exciting volume, and not just because it introduced a new theoretical scheme. For one thing, the vast historical range covered meant that theoretical claims stood out from historical detail. For another, the treatment of the migration of the leading edge of power from the Middle East to northwest Europe had great narrative thrust, taking the reader along in a dazzling excursus into world historical development. There were great incidental pleasures: an account of the way in which agriculture became prominent due to the early farmers' "caging" in the great river valleys; analysis of early empires, and in particular a sophisticated description of the rise and fall of Rome; the brilliant foray, based on an original concept of ideological power, into the emergence of the world religions; and an explanation for the rise to world power of the warring states of northwest Europe.

That first volume of *Sources* made his reputation, and saw him move from the London School of Economics to the University of California, where he still works. In contrast, the second volume, *The Rise of Classes and Nation-States, 1760–1914*, received rather less attention. The book is denser, filled with a mass of empirical detail; perhaps this demanded too much of readers unable to quickly grasp the varied originalities therein. The book continues to make use of his conceptualization of the four sources of power so as to trace again the leading edge of power, fundamentally through describing the interactions of the Great Powers of northwest Europe in the long nineteenth century. What is particularly striking about the volume are set pieces on key factors of social life—making the relative neglect shown to the volume astonishing, at least in my opinion. The chapters devoted to the modern state are the best available, an astonishing tour de force. Just as important is a careful explanation of the nature of class action, stressing the way in which social movements gain their character from the nature of the states with which they interact. Throughout the volume there is a subtle view of nationalism, albeit this is less clearly articulated than it is in key passages of the conversations that follow. And of course, the final chapter describes the moment at which Europeans began to lose their dominance in world historical terms. A case can be made that geopolitical competition between states inside the European sphere had led to progress overall—to the rationalization of states and the spread of economic and political innovation. But this very engine brought disaster once war was allied to industrial might.

Events interfere with academic plans as much as political programs. In the year that this second volume of *Sources* appeared Mann was challenged, at a Prague conference on nationalism organized by Ernest Gellner, about the ethnic cleansing then taking place in the Balkans. The result of this challenge was a huge diversion from the immediate completion of *Sources*, resulting in a pair of volumes—*Fascists* and *The Dark Side of Democracy: Explaining Ethnic Cleansing*—explaining the horrors of the twentieth century. These companion volumes certainly demonstrate the comparative historical sociological skills of a master of the genre. They were clearly hard to write. For the most impressive characteristic of both is the refusal to simply treat, or only treat, the perpetrators of horror as evil. Rather, sense had to be made of the actors involved; the rationality of their actions had to be appreciated and understood. This approach landed Mann in a good deal of trouble, particularly in the eyes of David Laitin, when speaking of "the dark side of democracy." It may be that the arresting nature of Mann's title was incautious given that liberal democracy has a relatively clean record as far as ethnic cleansing is concerned. But the title still seems to me brave and significant, forcing us to face the fact that normal people can act in repulsive ways—that ethnic cleansing can be popular and not, as is so often maintained, something engineered by manipulative political entrepreneurs.

There has been a second diversion from the continuation of *Sources*, albeit this too has done a great deal to enrich the concluding volume, to which we will turn in a moment. Since 1986 Mann has lived in the United States, inside the leading edge of world power, and he has thought more and more about its character. This is driven in part by his extreme dislike of that strand of its foreign policy that led to the invasion of Iraq. *Incoherent Empire* is a polemic against the imperial pretensions of the contemporary United States, suggesting that they are ill advised and doomed to failure. There is a certain amount of wobbling in Mann's position here, which we discuss below, much of it revolving around exactly when the primacy of the United States may be lost. For the second reason Mann concentrates so much attention on the United States is the widespread view that world politics are about to change. Only a few years ago there was much discussion of the unipolar moment of the United States; now all eyes turn to the way in which China, and perhaps India and Brazil, look set to add elements of multipolarity to the world polity.

The final volume of *Sources* is now complete, and it will appear in 2011. It is worth knowing that Mann has wobbled slightly when choosing a subtitle for this volume. The original subtitle was "Globalizations," referring to different processes that have drawn the world together. Those processes are present in the subtitle currently used, "Empires, Capitalism, and Nation-States"—although, as we see later, this too may be slightly amended. But the nature of the volume is neatly summed up by the following comments made in conversation in February 2010.

> In analyzing the world in the long twentieth century, up to today, the most fundamental social institutions have been capitalism, though contested by socialist and fascist modes of production, and nation-states, though at first the leading states also possessed empires and one of them still does. Thus, for example, globalization (a word that should really be pluraled) involves three main principles, the globalization of capitalism, the globalization of the nation-state, and the emergence of the first global empire, the American Empire. Capitalism generates class struggle, while nation-states and empires generate geopolitics, wars and sometimes civil wars. All generate ideologies, which in this period have been mainly secular rather than religious. These are the subject-matter of my most recent work.

Bearing these comments in mind—indeed, referring to them from time to time—will help readers orient themselves in this volume.

So a long intellectual journey has come to an end. The purpose of this book of interviews is to ask Mann about the social structures that constrain us and the options that are left to us in this not-so-new century. It should be made clear that attention does not focus on his final volume, although some of my questions reflect the fact that I read the manuscript early in 2010. Instead the attention is on contemporary circumstances, and on our life chances more generally. Of course, this involves critique, both positive and negative, so that the presuppositions of his work can be laid bare. My firm hope is that the interviews will illuminate his project as a whole, and encourage us to think about the nature of our times.

It may be of use to explain the manner in which this volume was created. The idea came from John Thompson of Cambridge University and of Polity Press, who was keen to hear more about the implications of Mann's recent work and of his project more generally, having been impressed by lectures that Mann has given over several summers in Cambridge. I have had the chance to engage with Mann's work over many years, and was delighted to be asked to engage with him in an assessment of the way in which he sees the forces of power at this point of time. An initial set of interviews, based on the divisions that structure this text, took place in February 2010 in Los Angeles. These form the core of this book. But there have been revisions. Readers may be amused to know that interviewing is rather messy, or at least it was in this case. Topics were raised on more than one occasion, with answers to early questions coming by means of digression at later stages. So revisions have reordered the text so as to gain cohesion and focus. And there have also been additions. A reading of the initial set of interviews made apparent some gaps in awareness and brought up questions that needed to be answered. Accordingly, some extra questions and answers in written form were added in July 2010. Despite all this, the character of the whole has been preserved. Occasionally, I have reverted to a topic when it seemed relevant in a different context, as happens in conversation; it is my hope that readers will appreciate these returns.

The ordering of the whole is apparent from the Table of Contents. Part One concentrates on the four sources of power at the core of Mann's sociological theory, to see how they have worked in the recent past and might work in the near future. Part Two turns to the character of social change, as it has affected us in the past and with an eye as to how it might affect us in the future. The initial intellectual division in the second part—a concern with countries and social groups as sources of change, followed by an examination of recent outcomes and an investigation into the patterns and contingencies at work in our world—is my own. But the stress on environmental matters comes from Mann himself. One can go a little further in this regard. In the early interviews Mann clearly wants to talk about environmental matters. An ironic paradox emerges at this point, at the end of all his labors. The final volume of *Sources* contains much material about progress. Europeans are seen as having escaped the horrors of their past, to a calmer, softer, less militaristic world. Yet at this moment of hope, a wholly new global problem has emerged which may be capable of undermining recent achievements. At the hour of success, disaster looms.

Part One

Powers in Motion

1

Capitalism

JAH: Let us begin this discussion of the sources of social power by considering matters economic. Your view seems to be that capitalism is now firmly entrenched as the dominant economic system of the age.

MM: Let me first briefly place capitalism amid the sources of social power. My overall claim is that there are four principal sources, ideological, economic, military, and political, and that in dealing with macro-sociological problems one must normally take all four into account. In analyzing the world in the long twentieth century, up to today, the most fundamental social institutions have been capitalism, though it has been contested by socialist and fascist modes of production, and nation-states, though at first the leading states also possessed empires and one of them still does. Thus, for example, globalization (a word that should really be plural) involves three main principles: the globalization of capitalism, the globalization of the nation-state, and the emergence of the first global empire, the American Empire. Capitalism generates class struggle, while nation-states and empires generate geopolitics, wars, and sometimes civil wars. All generate ideologies, which in this period have been mainly secular rather than religious. These are the subject matter of my most recent work, especially of Volume III of *The Sources of Social Power*, which I am currently finishing.

In answer to your specific question, yes, capitalism is very firmly entrenched in the modern world, and it has gotten more and more entrenched. As it has spread across the world, it has become the only economic power game in town. But capitalism has changed through time and comes in several varieties. In particular the rights of workers in the more advanced countries today are enormously greater than those in the nineteenth century. As capitalism has developed it has become more socially and legally constrained. Virtually the whole population has acquired what T. H. Marshall called "social citizenship," the right to share in the socioeconomic life of the nation—that is, within capitalism. Of course, it is still "capitalism" in the sense that there is private ownership of the means of production, the worker is separated from control of those means, and more and more of social life has been commodified, available for profit-seeking by capitalists.

JAH: But is capitalism also more entrenched in the sense that when it faced a considerable crisis in 2007 and 2008 it was possible to deal with that crisis much more effectively then had been the case in 1929?

MM: Maybe; it isn't over yet. But there are certainly two improvements over 1929. First, governments play a much larger role in regulation now than then, so it is easier for them to intervene with well understood policies, which have been around for a long time, and take short-term corrective action. Second, and perhaps more important, there is far more international collaboration of the organization of capitalism today

than in 1929. There were then competitive devaluations and tariffs in the 1930s which made it more
difficult for the world economy to recover. It is difficult
to say at the moment how quick the recovery will be,
but so far this seems like a great recession rather
than a Great Depression, and will likely not be as
significant as that of 1929. It is also more global in
the sense that it shifted a little bit the international
balance of power within the global economy, away
from the West, more toward Asia. Recovery is being
led by Asia, not by the West. This reveals that capitalism is more globally entrenched yet also more globally
varied.

JAH: Is it likely that capitalism will be more regulated after
this crisis, especially if it proves merely to be a great
recession? Banks in the United States were vulnerable
to regulation for a short period when Barack Obama
became President, but they now seem capable of resisting it.

MM: I expect a compromise there. I think banks are actually
a little more vulnerable to political backlash in the
United States than they are in Britain. Republicans and
Democrats alike counterpose "Wall Street" (the bad
guys) to "Main Street" (ordinary Americans). I expect
a little more regulation in the US. But despite this,
there is a third major difference between now and
1929: the absence now of substantial organized and
ideological opposition to capitalism. After 1929 there
were surges in both leftist and rightist opposition,
socialism and fascism. It is difficult to see parallels to
that right now, another sign of how much more
entrenched capitalism is. There will probably be a little
more regulation, varying somewhat between countries
though amid a little more international collaboration.
But as I said, we in the West have not solved capitalism's current problems.

The main problem now is the much greater role and power of finance capital, the increasing financialization of the economy. This means that governments with large debts and deficits feel the need to appease international finance capital. Their currencies or their bonds may be vulnerable to an attack. So they tailor policies toward the needs of bankers more than their citizens. To some extent this has always been true—we see it in the political economy of the 1920s, for example. But it is rampant right now. Keynesian-styled stimulus spending quickly gave way—in Europe at least—to deficit reduction and deflation to protect the value of the currency and the government bond. The first need is the security of the investor, and never mind about the resulting unemployment. And the banks themselves oppose much regulation. They think they have got the perfect solution already: they make lots of money in good times and when the bad times come they get bailed out and capitalism gets saved. So what could be better for them but worse for us?

JAH: If there is little new regulation, one can imagine a future in which new tools are created that again cause crisis—leading again to bailout.

MM: Yes, it seems very likely that there will be another crisis of a similar nature a few years down the road. We *should* be entering a phase of far more regulation of finance capital by government, but we might not get much of it. Power, not efficiency, rules the world—in my terms, distributive power dominates collective power—and this does not produce optimal results for the population as a whole. The US actually has the highest level of debt but because it is the reserve currency there is little speculative pressure against it. The Europeans—sterling and the euro, and especially the weaker economies of Europe—are under pressure. Governments are appeasing the speculators by introducing deflationary measures that include slashing government expenditures. Many economists think this will prolong the recession, but their advice is ignored.

Sovereign debt currently worries governments more than anything else. It is not impossible that we might now get a repeat of the Great Depression, when a stock market crash and some financial instability was intensified into real depression by government cutting of expenditure and tightening of credit. I think that Europe's conservative governments, in Britain, Italy, France, and Germany, are also taking advantage of the crisis to introduce welfare cuts that they have long wanted, but the basic pressure is coming from the markets, the movements of finance capital. It is bizarre that a financial crisis caused by neoliberalism should—after a short-term of Keynesian solutions—turn into more neoliberalism. It is even more bizarre that the United States, the real home (along with Britain) of neoliberalism, should warn the Europeans against this. It seems that the Americans have learned more lessons from this great recession than have the Europeans. But, I repeat, power, not efficiency, rules the world.

JAH: The contemporary absence of trade wars and competitive devaluations is, for sure, so different from the interwar period. Is there any likelihood of the emergence of regional trading blocs, with a consequent attack on free trade?

MM: I don't think it's very likely. It's just a possibility for the United States itself. One could envisage a backlash within the United States against international free trade, if the right kind of political coalition were put together, though it is so much against the interests of big American companies that I doubt it is going to happen. But if you think about the interdependence that is arising between Asia and the United States and Europe, and the important role of the overseas Chinese through Asia, you see that this is not a regionally segregated economy. About two-thirds of the globe is significantly interdependent, and some of this is simply transnational.

JAH: Is that the case because the United States still regulates capitalism? Does multilateral cooperation depend upon having a hegemonic leader?

MM: Not necessarily. It's true that in the postwar period the United States has been the leading power in international organizations, which have built up bit by bit. The World Trade Organization (WTO) now has legally binding restrictions on what countries can do in the way of tariffs and the like, to which the US is bound as well. Indeed, the US has been fined by the WTO. So there is something gradually building up that is more than just the United States, and indeed the kinds of economic things that the world blames the US for, such as structural adjustment programs, are done with the 100 percent collaboration of the Europeans. Sometimes the Japanese have deviated somewhat, but not the Europeans. If this is a hegemonic order, it's not just of the United States. It's also of international capitalism, especially finance capitalism, the most transnational form of capitalism. So I see it as kind of a dual hegemony—of both a class fraction and an American-led geopolitical alliance. The American part of this is also just beginning to be eroded. In particular we now see emerging an economic interdependence between the United States and China, plus Japan and the oil states. Countries other than the United States are pulling the world out of recession, especially China, whose manufacturing industry and exports are recovering.

JAH: So this is a mixed system. Nothing could happen without the United States because it has such a prominent role, but a multilateral element of agreement is needed to make it work?

MM: Yes, and that multilateralism is expanding. To the extent that there has been coordination, this has for almost the first time centered on the G20. It has been upgraded from a meeting of finance ministers to one of heads of state, and its composition reveals an extension of power from beyond the old West and Japan to the BRIC countries: Brazil, Russia, India, and especially China. That is a sign of movement in geopolitical power across the world.

JAH: There is a counterargument to what you have said. The United States retains enormous power, seen in its capacity to absorb most of the excess capital of the world economy. America might be weaker, but it's a peculiar sort of weakness where most other leading states seem determined to prop you up.

MM: That's true, and the shifts in power will take a long time. The dollar is going to remain a reserve currency for quite a while yet. There's no possible replacement for it. The euro has shown its weakness. It has no single directing force, other than the Bundesbank, which is not capable of leading a continent. Greece was bailed out, but mainly by Germany, and the process was politically fraught and far from automatic. More important, it is far from clear that a larger European national economy might receive such aid from Germany. And the Chinese currency is still controlled and restricted in various ways. The United States is going to remain the indispensible economic power for a while yet.

JAH: And nobody really has a fundamental interest in knocking the United States off its perch?

MM: No. The world economy benefits from a stable reserve currency and its principal actors are risk-averse. They do not want to go through what they fear would be a chaotic transition period from the dollar to a basket of currencies. That will eventually happen but most of the relevant power actors hope it will be slow and long-drawn-out.

JAH: So this situation does not resemble that of Great Britain at the beginning of the twentieth century, facing a major rival that had both economic and military power.

MM: That is correct, but in the British case, even before Germany became a serious threat, the pound as the reserve currency was being assisted by the other major banks, by the German bank, the Russian bank, the French bank. It had become a partly multilateral system, as Barry Eichengreen and others have shown, well before the rivalry with Germany became militarily threatening.

JAH: And the British case, in the end, is an example of being knocked off your perch by military exhaustion and huge debts incurred in war.

MM: Yes, not merely by any intrinsic logic of capitalist development, since that war was a product not of capitalism but of older great-power rivalry.

JAH: A further question about the United States concerns its remaining economic strength. Reports about patent-taking seem to suggest that at the higher end of product cycles the United States still does very well. Further, the United States has a notable capacity to absorb brain-power, most recently that of Indian engineers. Surely, American capitalism still looks rather strong?

MM: With patents I'm never quite sure if there is a bias in these statistics, since the Americans developed the patent system and rush to patent things immediately, so the quantity of the patents in the United States would dominate the world. I don't know the extent to which in reality the US dominates new and highly profitable technologies. I assume, like you do, that some American dominance results from its relatively open immigration policy and its fine universities. In US engineering faculties there are very few "Anglos," as they say, among the graduate students; they are substantially Asians and other foreign students, perhaps Asian-Americans or recent migrants, though most of them stay and become successful, and that is very important. If you see figures of the ethnic origins of the Nobel Prize winners, the United States is not the biggest per capita winner of Nobel Prizes—Sweden and Switzerland top the list.

JAH: Still, some of the Nobel Prize winners from Sweden, Switzerland, and elsewhere end up working in the United States.

MM: Exactly. There has also been considerable government assistance in the United States for high-tech industries. Part of it is military spinoff and part of it is just a federal government commitment to high tech. This doesn't fit well with the image of the United States as being a country of very little government regulation or intervention in industry. In the defense sector and high tech more generally there is a very high level of government sponsorship of R & D.

JAH: I have some questions about capitalist behavior. There is a sense in which your works suggests disappointment in capitalists: they spend their time making money, and lack larger geopolitical visions. Have you changed your mind about that?

MM: Well, I wouldn't go quite as far as you've said, but I think I would view their behavior along those lines.

Of course, there are institutions of collaboration among capitalists, like think tanks and the World Economic Forum, and some of the major industries do plan years ahead, like the energy industry, for example. But I don't see them playing a large role in geopolitics and in foreign policy unless firms have their own bottom line in view. In foreign policies relating to particular countries there are business lobbies. But overall, I don't see the directions of foreign policy being determined by the views or interests of capitalism as a whole.

JAH: The other way I can put this issue to you is to say that the world might be safer if it thought more in terms of economic advantage and disadvantage. That is a softer language than that of pure power, which has ended up killing so many more people.

MM: I think that is to an extent true, at least of advanced or successfully developing countries, though across large swathes of the world capitalists are using coerced forms of labor. But capitalists are dealing with inputs and outputs which are calculable and they obviously try very hard to calculate profit and loss, so they engage in more rational behavior than do state elites and political constituencies mobilized by the elites. There has been so much emotion-driven irrationality in foreign policy in the long twentieth century, and it continues today in the case of the United States and its enemies. I tend to see that in most cases few capitalists have wanted war. Had the state listened to capitalists they wouldn't have gone into so many wars.

JAH: I'd like to take a step backwards, away from this moment of triumph for the capitalist model, to ask about the failure of socialism. Should we conclude than nonmarket systems simply do not work?

MM: Well, first there is a long line of research stretching from Dieter Senghaas through Linda Weiss and John Hobson to Ha-Joon Chang and Atul Kohli showing that successful economic development, with the possible exception of eighteenth- and nineteenth-century Britain, has never been entirely the result of free markets. From early Germany and the United States to Japan and the East Asian Tigers to India, the most rapidly developing capitalist economies have all enjoyed a high level of government protection, incentives, and overall coordination.

It is also the case that state socialism enjoyed a fair measure of economic success during its heyday in the catch-up phase of industrialization. The Soviet Union from the 1930s to the 1960s grew its GDP more than any other country in that period except for Japan. And China's later growth "grew out from the plan," as Barry Naughton has shown. Of course, we must set that success against the terrible atrocities wrought especially on peasants by Stalin's forced collectivization and Mao's Great Leap Forward. GDP growth achieved at the cost of millions dead is not a benefit to its citizens. However, both regimes did at least learn not to do such things again, and Vietnam learned from them how to grow without massive atrocities. The first and second industrial revolutions had seemed to map out quite well what a desirable economic future would be so that centralized planning could help bring it about. It specifically required surpluses to be taken from agriculture and invested in industry, and authoritarian governments had some advantages in that respect. In the industrializing period state socialism paid off.

But the Soviet regime never managed to get beyond the industrial phase into post-industrialism, to which centralized state planning seems less appropriate. Its economy was stagnating from the 1970s onward. China and Vietnam then learned from this to decentralize and marketize while still retaining some measure of central control. We don't know yet whether the consequent boost in growth will continue within their present framework of highly mixed forms of property ownership, or whether they will move into a variant form of capitalism. But Schumpeter argued that capitalism excelled at what he called "creative destruction," the ability to shift gears to go through crisis into a new economic phase, and that does seem to be the distinctive ability of a decentralized, competitive economy such as capitalism.

But the world perceives something much simpler than this—that socialism failed and capitalism succeeded, period. That perception has much more force in the world than any more nuanced judgment. So socialism as centralized planning is almost dead as an ideal. But my own final judgment is different: that its *political* failure was much clearer than its economic failure. Socialist revolution brought swift and seemingly inevitable degeneration into authoritarianism since it never possessed any mechanisms by which an all-conquering revolutionary elite would cede power to more democratic forces.

JAH: But is capitalism really the only game in town? The success of contemporary China seems to suggest a greater future for state-directed political economies than you allow.

MM: Capitalism is *almost* the only game in town. The Chinese game is a little different, since it combines much centralized planning by a ruling communist party with enterprises acting fairly autonomously on markets, which are themselves mixtures of private property and local officials' de facto property. It is not yet capitalism and it may not even be on the road to capitalism. Chinese institutions that might seem capitalist, like the stock exchange, do not operate autonomously and are substantially phony. The Party has shown in the last two years that it can, at the flick of a switch, move massive resources into infrastructure projects and alternative energy technologies in a way that governments in capitalist economies cannot. It is not state capitalism in Trotsky's sense since the economy is not controlled by a unified state elite. The Party has actually lost control of many of its officials who are making money out of their effective possession of enterprises, though this is often shared with people who really are capitalist. I call this heterogeneous regime the "Capitalist Party-State." It controls over 10 percent of the world economy, a percentage that will likely double over the next two decades.

I think most Chinese would regard its transition away from state socialism as being pretty close to optimal. Most would wish to have more children and ideally they would like more civil and political freedoms, but they seem willing to trade these for growing prosperity while maintaining social order. This combination is most threatened by massively growing inequality, between town and country, between regions, and between classes. At the top the Party is aware of the need to reverse these trends but it is unclear if they will be able to do much, given their commitment to growth and their loss of control over their own cadres.

JAH: Is this to be contrasted to the way in which the market spread within postcommunist societies?

MM: For Russia it is a different story. Here the transition was to capitalism. It was also rapid and involved wholesale seizure of public assets by private individuals, especially by former Party and NKVD apparatchiks.

It brought not growth but collapse at first, and then it brought only growth based on natural energy resources. And it brought massive inequality. Putin is popular because he provided minimal order out of much chaos and because he seemed to be taking on the new capitalist oligarchs. Neoliberals played a considerable role in this story of failure, though one must concede that Russia's transition was much more difficult than China's since its economy was dominated by inefficient industrial behemoths. Neoliberals respond to accusations of failure by saying that their models were never fully applied. The latter part of the statement is true, since pragmatic politicians realized they could never stay in power if they did introduce the whole neoliberal package.

But the Soviet-Russia transition reveals the failure of models that regard economic modes of production as primary and self-sustaining rather than having preconditions emanating from the other sources of social power. In this case political power was crucial. The Chinese Communist Party retained political power and managed a transition, to great effect. In contrast, the Soviet Communist Party was deliberately dismantled. It then collapsed and there was a botched transition.

JAH: What does this tell us about the chances of development for poorer countries within the newly dominant capitalist world order?

MM: We can obviously be more optimistic now than at most points in the last forty years. Many countries are now achieving some growth. It is not just the much-publicized BRICs, but also the whole of Southeast Asia, Eastern Europe, Turkey, and even some African countries such as South Africa, Botswana, Uganda, Algeria, and Nigeria. After the failures of both "African socialism" and neoliberalism, it seems that a mixed economy mode of state-coordinated capitalist development, varying according to local resources, might be more legitimate and more successful, though obviously not in uniform fashion across the world. We might be shifting finally into a near-global economy.

JAH: I have one final question. To what extent are we really talking about capitalism in any case? Surely the system as a whole is American-dominated? Isn't it worth remembering that both Karl Polanyi and Maynard Keynes stressed the way in which markets are made by states?

MM: It remains capitalism, though in the advanced countries it is a reformed capitalism, one from which rights for workers and for the community have been wrested. It is only partially American, for it actually contains three principal elements: transnational, national (and therefore also international), and American imperial. Indeed, a fourth element often surfaces, the "macroregional," so that the capitalisms of the Nordic countries or the Anglophone countries share a certain style. There is a big debate about "varieties of capitalism" that has not yet been resolved. But I think it is safe to say that there are certain national and macro-regional styles that withstand some of the pressures imposed by the tendency of capitalism to escape all national boundaries, and by the dollar and US dominance of some international agencies.

Some variations through time are also evident, and the tension between plan and market sometimes appears to have a cyclical element, as Polanyi noted. This is not quite as regular as he suggested, however, for it comes from rather specific processes of interstitial emergence in each period, and it is not clear that these are actually solved by more state regulation. The

1920s were beset by the entwining of economic and geopolitical crises; the 1970s by the interstitial emergence of transnational finance capital networks; and the early twenty-first century will be beset by the unexpected environmental destructiveness of capitalism. The first crisis was managed by more regulation summed up in the word "Keynesian"; the second crisis is still with us, and capitalist market interests are fighting a very strong battle against more state regulation; and the third crisis might end with disaster, not planning. But we will talk about this particular crisis later.

2

Militarism

JAH: The word "revolution" is much abused, and certainly overused. But in military affairs, there has been a genuine revolution. Do you agree that the creation of nuclear weapons has fundamentally changed the nature of war?

MM: Yes, it has. And this is a case where a major crisis was more or less solved with great success. Atomic and hydrogen bombs were the first really sociologically significant thing about globalization. Globalization is occurring and is important, but it is for the most part not particularly sociologically interesting because it involves the expansion of all the social structures that we've analyzed in the past. If you look at the literature on globalization it still concerns classes, enterprises, states, demographic transitions, idealism versus materialism, major structural identities against multiple identities, and so on. Yet if human activity fills up the world and then rebounds back against human society rather like a boomerang, transforming the conditions of action, then we need distinctive theories. At that point globalization itself has become causally important. Weapons that could destroy the world constitute the first example of this, and anthropomorphic climate change constitutes the second boomerang effect.

Nuclear weapons changed the nature of war and of many states. It didn't mean there wouldn't be any more wars, because human beings are not always rational. We might have had a nuclear war but there was just enough restraint by state elites to avoid it. This was the great global crisis that didn't happen, which was averted, the one great success for humanity as compared to the Great Depression, a great recession and two world wars. Great good sense was shown in the emerging conduct of American and Soviet leaders during the Cold War. When they reached dangerous levels of confrontation it terrified them and they reacted. First Kennedy and Krushchev during the Cuban Missile Crisis, then Reagan and Gorbachev after the panicky Soviet reaction to NATO's Able Archer war-game in 1983. Of course, it was easier for them to understand each other because there were only two of them. There were no chains of action and unanticipated reaction as there were in the case of the multiple great powers who caused the two world wars. It was also easier in that the threat of nuclear war itself, unlike the rest of the Cold War, did not invoke the rivalry between capitalism and socialism. War would have overwhelmed them both. So they could focus exclusively on a singular, potentially devastating threat.

Indeed, nuclear weapons have so far disciplined leaders into rationality. Countries that have acquired nuclear weapons have tended to subsequently moderate their foreign policies, as in the cases of India and Pakistan— another simple, dual confrontation. These are not the only causes of the radical reduction in the incidence of inter-state warfare which has occurred since 1950, but they have been very important. The backbone of most relatively advanced states is no longer the fiscal-military nexus that scholars like Charles Tilly and myself emphasized for earlier times. That is the best news coming out of the second half of the twentieth century.

It also brings a major change in social causation. In the first half of the twentieth century, social development was profoundly affected by mass mobilization warfare. Without the two world wars, probably no fascist or communist regimes (only failed revolutions), no massive American Empire, no single reserve currency, less variable rhythms of the development of social citizenship in the liberal countries, perhaps no nuclear power and who knows what other technologies, perhaps more multi-ethnic states, perhaps no grand social democratic / Christian democratic compromise in continental Europe—though as I go on these become less confident counter-factuals, and all would have to be carefully qualified (as I do in Volume III). Sociologists have preferred a much simpler evolutionary story of the growth of capitalism, democracy, and the nation-state succeeded by globalization, but they can only perform such theoretical feats by imposing simplifying pacific blinkers on their view of the world. Now, if we had a major war, it could destroy the world or substantial parts of it. But without such a war, maybe we can for the first time have simpler, more rational, more peaceable models of social development.

JAH: Yet one issue that remains before the world is the possibility of nuclear proliferation. You've argued that Iran is likely to want nuclear weapons because the United States doesn't attack countries that possess them, as has been true of North Korea. Hence it is very likely that more countries will surely get them. The possession of a few nuclear weapons is senseless, at least in pure logic, for their use would bring on total extermination. Does that make you optimistic about nuclear weapons? Or do nuclear weapons still scare you dreadfully? They were used twice and they have not been used since. Do you fear they could be used again?

MM: Proliferation means we have to rely on the rationality of more and more world leaders. It would never be rational to launch one's nuclear weapons, since it invites an immediate devastating retaliation. But there are two nightmare scenarios. One is that leaders who are so committed to an ideology, in Weber's terms being "value-rational" (pursuing one goal to the detriment of all other considerations) might, if in deep trouble, launch nuclear (or biological or chemical) weapons. The other possibility is that the weapons could be stolen and used by a nonstate group similarly pursuing value-rationality, such as Al Qaeda. These are worries for politicians today, and they are right to be worried, but the best solution would be to buy off or make friends with the potential proliferators. Only states feeling threatened have developed nuclear weapons. It is within the capacity of the United States and its allies to solve this problem, though in the Middle East it would require radical policy changes.

JAH: In terms of military power, we are in a strange situation. The Great Powers have weapons of catastrophic power, but they can't be used. So has the military balance in the world fundamentally changed, or is it still the case that the Great Powers have the military edge?

MM: Even unable to use their nuclear weapons, the Great Powers, especially the US, have the military edge—to put it mildly. The United States has more potent weapons at almost every level of technology than any potential adversary. It spends 48 percent of the military expenditure of the entire world. If we add its allies' spending, that rises to about 73 percent. It has a near-monopoly of the new generation of high-tech weapons systems. And the US can strike any adversary from its extraordinary global network of bases (as Chalmers Johnson has emphasized). Not even China would wish to risk war with the US.

The US can devastate but the question is whether this is a particularly useful military capacity. What is it meant to achieve? It is not merely a matter of self-defense. That could be done with a military well under half its present size. The intent is much more expansionist. It is first to secure sufficient of the world's resources for its own economy to keep on growing, and here oil and natural gas are the main priorities. Again, however, the best way to get oil is surely to make friends with the oil producers (and the US does do this selectively, though only with conservative regimes). But second, in traditional imperial fashion, the US wants to bend other countries to its will. The best possible construction of this goal is the view put forward by America's leaders that this would make the world a better place by inducing regime changes, especially in hostile countries, to make them more peaceful and more democratic.

This is, of course, a traditional form of imperial mission statement. The Romans said they brought order and justice to the conquered; the Spanish, the Word of God; the British, free trade; the French, *la mission civilisatrice*; and now the Americans, democracy and free enterprise. It is not generally understood abroad that this is the view not just of the recent Bush the Younger administration but of the entire American geopolitical establishment. Article after article in *Foreign Affairs*, its main journal, argues from the assumption that there is an "American responsibility"

for "world order." Though there is obviously disagreement over how many military interventions this should
involve, and whether the US can bring democracy to
the world, and some inside the Beltway do believe that
the "war on terror" is counter-productive, no one
doubts that the US should have overwhelming military
force which must be put in service of laudable goals.

Can these goals be achieved? Yes, but only if there is
genuine consensus that a genocide or some lesser form
of mass killing should and could be stopped by the use
of overwhelming force. In the present world, such an
intervention if launched against anything other than
the puniest of powers would virtually have to be led
by the United States. However, the "could" involves
having an alternative local government enjoying
popular support ready to put in place of the deposed
regime. The Vietnamese army successfully invaded
Cambodia, overthrew the Khmer Rouge, ended its
mass murders, and installed a client government with
enough popular support to rule stably. They did so
because the Khmer Rouge had been killing the Vietnamese minority in Cambodia and then even had the
temerity to invade a stretch of Vietnamese territory.
The US-led NATO interventions in the former Yugo-
slavia also had popular local Bosniak and Albanian
Kosovan regimes to install afterwards.

But this major requirement is not often met. The
American power to overcome regimes cannot be
doubted. Even if we think that the Iraq invasion of
2003 was a disaster, Saddam Hussein and his cronies
were overthrown and killed, and so one might think
that other hostile countries would draw the obvious
lesson and be wary about antagonizing the United
States—though it doesn't apparently deter Iran. One
must also doubt whether the American military dominance is actually achieving much beyond intimidation.

Is there a better regime installed in Iraq now? The number of Iraqi casualties incurred by the invasion and occupation probably equals or exceeds the number of Saddam's victims, and there is also more ethnic/religious instability now. Iraq has elections but they are ethnic/religious plebiscites concerning which group will control the country. Nor is the US getting more oil or controlling the oil industry. Most important, the invasion and occupation increased the terrorist threat rather than being an effective answer to it, as is also the case in the continuing occupation of Afghanistan, an obviously hopeless case.

There is one basic reason for this failure, which I put forward in my book *Incoherent Empire*. Empire is no longer legitimate, as American leaders know full well, since they vehemently deny they are imperialists. Nationalism is the world's dominant ideology, and that includes an ideal of national self-determination that precludes invasions by foreign powers. Intervention was possible and sometimes popular in Cold War days when the US could always find local allies who preferred capitalism to socialism. Actually, the Third World Left usually only wanted social democracy, but they weren't allowed that either. Now that ideological dimension is rarely present. Collaborators with the US are denounced locally as traitors to the nation (and sometimes also as apostates). In Iraq, the most loyal allies have been the Kurds, but their loyalty is strictly conditional on getting their own nation-state (with oil resources) which they are indeed achieving. But their own political processes, not the US, will determine whether their regime is democratic and whether they have "free enterprise."

The US has the military power to destroy but it does not have the political or ideological power to reconstruct. But as yet virtually no American politician and very few Washington think-tank intellectuals accept that. "Responsibilities" get in the way and "loss of face" through withdrawal is also considered unacceptable. Emotion-laden status concerns are important in geopolitics, making leaders prefer war to "backing down." Afghanistan in this respect may do for Obama what Vietnam did for Lyndon Johnson. Is it not remarkable that at this time of fiscal crisis, when politicians cry out that deficits must be reduced, that American politicians of both parties promise not to introduce cuts into this extraordinarily oversized military? The War on Terror has become so entrenched, and so mixed up with emotional fears for status and security, that we're not finished with war yet, even though it has become largely irrational.

JAH: However, it's still the case that the United States can afford this military. The cost is perhaps a trillion dollars annually if you include hidden payments for the CIA and special funding for the wars. But that is one trillion out of an economy of fourteen or fifteen trillion dollars. This is far less as a proportion of GDP than was the case during the Korean War, or than Soviet military spending at any time. And some of that money goes into high-tech investment. If you cut it you would have economic problems because of the diminution of military Keynesianism involved. All in all, I do not see that its commitment to military affairs is crowding out its economic success.

MM: It can afford it as long as foreign capital keeps coming into the United States, and as long as the dollar seigniorage pays for it. Otherwise Americans would have to pay higher taxes in order to pay for it, and that might be politically impossible. In the meantime, as you say, the US can easily afford it, though it could also just as easily cut it. Most economists say it is not necessary for economic growth—military Keynesianism has not been operative for decades. In the 1990s the American military was reduced by almost a third and it didn't have any serious effects on the economy. It could be done again, but at the moment it won't be, since Americans want to feel safe and do not appreciate how safe they actually are, and how simpler, less costly alternative policies could make them even safer. Another reason is that military spending is politically entrenched. When the Pentagon proposes any big new military program, it deliberately spreads the various research, production, and base facilities involved across as many states and Congressional districts as possible. The B-2 bomber was produced in 22 states. That brings more votes on the Hill.

JAH: Of course, the figures do mislead in one important way. An American soldier in the field is a very, very expensive proposition, whereas an Afghan in the hills, with much more limited weapons, is really very cheap indeed. So is it the case that the weak have significant capacities of resistance against this huge military machine?

MM: At present each month those Afghan fighters are managing to inflict more and more casualties on NATO troops—in 2010 over 700, the highest annual figure since the occupation started in 2001. In fact in the whole post-WWII period guerillas have done remarkably well against better-armed states. Martin van Creveld has shown this. But you are right that the American soldier is extremely expensive. One reason is that there are far fewer combat troops proportionately than in other armed forces in the world. Underlying this is an extremely high level of protection of the American soldier. The US doesn't want to send its soldiers into dangerous situations. Their lives are sacred. The number of times that they match guerillas with low-intensity warfare of their own is extremely limited. If you get in fire-fights, you call in the air strikes. In fact, it is curious that we never quite had this kind of military power before: where America fights wars, and the public seems to more or less support it, but rejects the idea that its citizens be killed. It is spectator-sport militarism. This leads to what is perhaps the major weakness of the United States: the enemy's accurate belief that if it simply outlasts us it will win. Eventually we withdraw because we can't take the casualties. That is already becoming true in Afghanistan, as it was in Iraq, for some of the NATO allies. It is only a military weakness. It's a normative strength, a sign of a civilized country.

JAH: So America can shock and awe, but in the end it can't control because it does not have enough boots on the ground to actually restructure a situation?

MM: It can overthrow regimes, but it can't restructure. And it is less a question of the number of boots than of ideological and political legitimacy.

JAH: I have a slightly different set of questions about military power. You often use the word "militarism." I think that you use it in two senses. Most obviously, you suggest that the military element in society can have a certain measure of autonomy. You could see this in the past in the introduction of a new military technology like chariots, and at the end of the nineteenth century you've certainly shown the autonomy of certain officer corps not controlled by states. But you also use "militarism" to describe an attitude that says that war is viable, even desirable. Is it accurate to say that you have used the word in two different ways?

MM: That may be so. Autonomous military castes, which form your first sense of militarism, mostly occur nowadays in less advanced countries. We especially see them in Africa and to a declining extent in South and Central America and the Middle East. Many scholars have analyzed such regimes and I have little to say about them that is new. But in Volume III I tend to use the term in the second, more pejorative sense in contexts where it is not generally used, such as to describe European society in 1914 or recent US policy. These are "militaristic," in the sense of having a high valuation of military power, using it as what I call the "default mode of diplomacy." There is no other word than "militarism" which quite conveys such a high valuation of military power.

In such contexts leaders and sometimes the masses as well regard war as a normal and even honorable solution to foreign-policy problems. In the United States today people certainly don't like the term used for their country, but when the country has been needlessly at war for almost a whole decade, killing hundreds of thousands of civilians, refusing to reduce a grotesque level of military expenditure, they need to be shocked into recognizing that this is an accurate description of their country—and not at all how civilized countries should behave.

JAH: The reason I am concerned with this is simple. There are certainly military elites which are autonomous and which like to fight, but there are other occasions when soldiers, who after all get killed in combat, are actually more cautious than some civilians. What comes to mind for me is the opposition between the militarism of the romantic civilian intellectuals prominent in the early years of the last Bush's presidency in contrast to the relative caution shown by Colin Powell, a former soldier—although his resistance to those intellectuals didn't last that long. I sometimes think that the greatest militarists are romantic, geopolitically inclined intellectuals.

MM: I don't think it's only intellectuals. It is also politicians. Just before the First World War German, French, British, and Russian statesmen didn't make militaristic-sounding speeches, but war mobilization was high on their list of possible diplomatic moves, and they believed war was very useful to attain policy objectives. They were used to routinely fighting wars in the colonies. Between them the British, French and Dutch fought over 100 separate wars between 1870 and 1914, almost all in their colonies, and European children read adventure stories lauding the heroism of soldiers, sailors, and colonial administrators. War was normalized in this culture.

As to the generals, sometimes they are cautious, sometimes not. Japanese officers led Japan's surge into China and the Pacific War. McArthur led his soldiers to pee in the Yalu River, provoking Chinese retaliation in Korea. American generals in Vietnam wanted the gloves off against North Vietnam. It is true that Colin Powell enshrined a very cautious "Powell Doctrine" and that in the administration of Bush the Younger, generals had to be purged before Bush's policy could be implemented. That was also true among Hitler's generals. But soldiers as a whole are not more wary of war. It is what they are trained to do, and it is how they get promotion and status, how they prove that they are indispensible.

JAH: This leads me to a general comment about a change in your work over the years: you've completely fallen out with militarism.

MM: That's perfectly true in modern times, when war has become too destructive to be useful. It also makes me reflect on what I wrote about the Roman Empire, for example. Was I too positive about its military accomplishments? On the other hand, what I stressed then was the Roman legion as an engineering corps, assisting economic development. I also emphasized the Roman willingness to confer citizenship on those it conquered. In contrast, the racism of modern empires prevented them generally granting citizenship to conquered peoples. And apart from the short-lived and otherwise rather harsh Japanese Empire and the white settler colonies that committed mass murder on the native populations, economic development is not something associated with modern empires.

JAH: But then there is Tacitus recording Calgacus, a British chieftain, speaking to his men before battle: "To robbery, slaughter, plunder, they give the lying name of empire; they make a solitude and call it peace."

MM: The initial phase of conquest is the downside of all empires. But Roman rule then became a lot more beneficent than British or French rule ever did.

JAH: I have a final general question. Your account of social change in previous eras stressed the impact of military competition—the need to tax and conscript, consequentially leading to counter-mobilizations of one sort or another. Are you now arguing that this source of social dynamism has lost salience? What might that mean?

MM: I would now stress more than ever the importance of fiscal-military competition between many small states as a key to the "European Miracle" in the early modern period. It enabled the Europeans to go out and conquer much of the world, while in Europe it led to popular counter-mobilizations demanding no taxation without representation. Whether imperialism did anyone any good in the colonies is another matter. But in the end their militarism led the Europeans (and the Japanese) to geopolitical downfall in the twentieth century.

World wars, nuclear weapons, and the continuing development of military technology more or less ended the role of military competition in general social development. Military Keynesianism hasn't worked since the Korean War. In poorer countries the postwar rise in civil wars, thankfully leveling off during the 1990s, was simply bad news for those countries. War no longer has anything positive to offer beyond a few cases where it might be the lesser of two evils.

3

Political Power

JAH: It is very noticeable that your view of the long twentieth century concentrates as much on the dialectic
between empires and nation-states as it does on the
triumph of the capitalist model. Am I right to say that
you think that the imperial moment can never be
created again, that the nation-state is the predominant
political form throughout the world?

MM: I would qualify that, since the United States still
does have an empire. It is the only surviving empire,
the only global empire there has ever been. It is
in some ways the most powerful, especially in military power, but in others it is weak compared to
most historical empires, principally because it has
lost ideological legitimacy and political support
among those it can conquer. It hasn't declined yet.
But it will decline, especially when the dollar is no
longer the world's reserve currency. World systems
theorists who have predicted its decline for decades
will be right eventually. Then we will have a system of
nation-states in which the US will remain the most
powerful. But then, nation-state systems are inherently
unequal.

JAH: There are obviously different levels to imperial power. It is possible to talk about a world system, say in the British case. Great Britain derived enormous economic benefits from Argentina, which was not formally part of the Empire; and had the loyal white Dominions, colonies that held shared nationalist sentiments; then the crucial case of India; and endless African colonies subject to indirect rule. The United States is a little bit like that in a way, isn't it?

MM: We must be precise about what kind of empire the US has. All empires have contained different modes of rule. It is conventional among historians to distinguish direct, indirect, and informal types of empire. These are ideal types since real empires characteristically blend together two or three of them, according to region. The first two types contain colonies; the third does not. To this conventional model I have added different types of informal empire, depending on whether power is exercised through military or economic means, and then we must add hegemony, a lighter form of rule that is not experienced as coercive or therefore imperial. The essence of empire is the notion of a core and a periphery, with the core subordinating and intimidating the periphery.

The United States suddenly acquired a partially global empire because of World War II (and Hitler's folly). But in its postwar relations with Europe and Japan, and later with East Asia as well, it did not really coerce. It has been in those regions the accepted leader so has been a hegemonic not an imperial power. It is true there is an element of economic coercion, since other countries subsidize the United States through the dollar, and they know that. But they accept it as the way the world works.

JAH: This is the price that has to be paid when one lacks military autonomy!

MM: But even now when there isn't really a threat to Europe, the Europeans are willing to pay because it is the way that their capitalism works, too; it's a part of their own system. But the United States has in other parts of the world maintained military force. It has intervened repeatedly, sometimes covertly, sometimes overtly, backed up by that extraordinary global American base system whose purpose is to intimidate. And so I think that the United States remains imperial, even though over parts of the world its rule is no longer coercive. In Asia there has been a trend toward less coercion. The United States fought two major wars, the Korean and Vietnam wars, but the long-term result has been the pacification of the region and its integration into a world economy that the United States leads. The communist states were never a part of this dominion, of course, and China still isn't a part, and there are other important states that are fairly autonomous, like India or Indonesia. So it is not quite a global empire.

JAH: This is an occasion when I'd like to ask again about American power, essentially because I see it as potentially resilient. Even if you were right before to say the burden of empire might cause problems, surely there is something to the view that the United States can change its foreign policy. It lost the war in Vietnam, but that country is now entering the world capitalist system! Why not an ever more nonterritorial form of empire, control at lower cost? So if the United States doesn't have foolish military ventures, why can its imperial reach not last?

MM: The American Empire can last for a while yet but in the long run its relative decline in economic weight will threaten its general level of power. There was of course a relative decline from 1950, a point in time when the US had possessed an extraordinarily proportion of the world economy, but this then stabilized in the 1970s until the present at about 20–25 percent of world GDP. But right now it is just beginning to go down because of the successful development of other countries. The weight of India and China is beginning to have an impact on all such percentages. Eventually the reserve currency will be not the dollar but a basket of currencies including the dollar. Not yet, not for twenty years, perhaps. It's at that point that America will have to start asking questions about whether it can afford this military, and whether it achieves significant goals. Unless the Chinese change their spots and become more aggressive militarily, I would expect American empire to decline. If China became more militaristic then other Asian countries might well turn to the United States for help, and then overall there would be a continuation of hegemony more than empire. But there would be conflict ensuing within those countries, and the US would probably intervene in suppressing groups that were opposed to the new military defense of Asia against China—just as in the Cold War.

JAH: In China itself, it is sometimes said that young intellectuals—especially students, of whom there are very large numbers—resent the power of the United States. There were demonstrations at the time the Chinese embassy in Belgrade was hit by an American missile during the last Balkan wars. Such intellectuals would like China to more forcefully represent itself in the world. So there are Chinese nationalists inside China. In Europe there's a certain amount of resentment, a sort of whining against the United States, but it has no consequence. Is it possible that resentments in China, a rising power, might lead to something stronger?

MM: Well, it's certainly possible but mainly because there is a lightning rod for conflict to focus on—Taiwan.

Overwhelmingly, the mainland Chinese think that Taiwan is part of China, while American support of Taiwan has always been a little bit ambiguous. I simply don't know what might happen there. All three governments have reason to be very cautious, though it would be different if the US began to back away from Taiwan. China is also expanding across Africa, seeking its natural resources, though so far this is entirely peaceful and indeed many Africans welcome China as the only truly noncolonial power active in Africa. The Chinese avoid any criticism of African regimes and will deal with the worst rights violators among them. At some point the United States might take alarm at Chinese expansion, so one cannot be sure that there will be an era of world peace. Any threat of confrontation would bring the Europeans and Japan begging for American protection.

JAH: The nation-state principle affects the United States whenever it is involved in intervention because that principle produces nationalist reactions rather quickly. The idea that invaders would be welcomed is now wrong nearly all the time, unless the invaders can count on some local people, like the Kurds, whose support is based on what they can get out of the invasion. So why is the nationalist principle so powerful, why has it become so dominant? Why does your book posit the nation-state as the political form that is going to survive? In the background to my question is the thought of Ernest Gellner, whom we both knew. His functionalist theory stressed that the nation-state was an area of communication that helped industrial organization. Is that a strong theory? I don't think it was correct.

MM: Ernest was right in seeing nationalism as essentially modern. But I see it less as a functionalist response to industrialization than as the unintended consequence of the tightening networks of industrial capitalism and of the demands for political liberties among the peoples of the multi-ethnic authoritarian empires. Key was resistance to the tax-gatherers and recruiting sergeants whose depredations were generated by more and more expensive wars. As rule by the people became the general demand, the notion of the people as a nation strengthened—if there was some communality of history, like a language shared by elites or a prior history of political independence or substantial provincial rule (for nations were not created out of thin air). Then resistance to the empires became known as "nationalism." Sometimes outside of Europe the demand was in reality more racial, against "white" rule, but the nation-state—sovereignty over a given territorial area by or in the name of the people—became the hegemonic ideal everywhere, and so did the "nation."

JAH: Let's think of nationalism, and then liberal democracy afterwards. Has nationalism been so successful already that its work is in effect done? Can you imagine there being any more states now, or do you think that the states that are present now will be able to nationalize their territories? After all, the great waves of nation-state creation came at the back of the collapse of empires. There are no more empires, so perhaps it won't have that historic effect again.

MM: First the historical issue: we sometimes call movements "nationalist" when really they were nothing of the kind. When we talk about "African nationalism," for example, that is not really an accurate label, for it was a racial protest movement against the white colonial power. They usually accepted that the existing colony would be their territory and demanded its liberation. But the notion that this might be a nation was almost completely fictional. Their own identity was racial rather than national. But as they developed their state they tried to develop a national identity and a nation-state. Since they thought that successful countries were nation-states, they sought to emulate them. In the second half of the nineteenth century, the multinational states perished, the ones that were clearly multinational. The Soviet Union held on longest. But now we have 192 self-styled nation-states—and the American Empire.

As to what's happened recently and what will happen after that great phase of nation creation, the answer is so far very little change. Most attempts at restructuring were not aiming at larger multinational states but at the secession of a smaller purported nation. They have been mostly unsuccessful because the existing states of the region, especially in Africa, have a common interest in suppressing them. A few states might break up in the future, like the Ukraine, Belgium, or the Sudan. The interesting thing about the European Union is how you can actually have quite well developed supranational institutions, and at the same time the nation-state doesn't wither away. Indeed, there have been internal nationalist reactions against the European Union. So I think that the nation-state will remain the dominant political form in the foreseeable future. It is buttressed by many institutions, from tax and welfare systems to international sporting rivalry. These are taking over from war as their main purpose, changing their nature, hopefully into more peaceable ways.

JAH: I would like to just go back for a moment to your claim that one of the reasons that nationalism spreads is that people regard it as the leading form of power, and so want to copy it. But at the beginning of the twentieth century, the nation copied was Britain, which was a nation with an empire. If the Russians could manage to make Ukrainians into little Russians, there would be more than 50 percent ethnic civil Russians inside a czarist empire. There is a sense in which they were trying to become this odd thing, an imperial nation-state. Surely the age of nationalism in a sense comes very late? Of course, the way World War I ends certainly creates nations, but the British empire extends itself at that very time—with real collapse only becoming apparent during World War II, on account of promises made to gain Indian loyalty together with defeat at the hands of the Japanese.

MM: These states were dual, nation-states at home, empires abroad, the former becoming democratic, the latter not at all, except for white settler colonies. Empires contracted significantly as a result of World War I. It's true that like the French and Belgians the British acquired UN-mandated territories after World War I, but they acquired them from the defeat of the German and Ottoman Empires. The successor states after World War I were mainly in Eastern Europe and they became simple nation-states themselves, partly as a result of ethnic cleansing of minorities. After World War I British and French politicians, especially on the Right, overestimated the durability of their empires. They could certainly count on their settler colonies, but besides them only India contributed much to their cause in World War II, and India had to be bribed to do so. The fact that the other Asian colonies fell so easily to the Japanese, sometimes with local complicity, indicates that British, French, and Dutch power in Asia was quite limited. The hostility of the League of Nations to interwar Italian and Japanese imperialism also reveals that national self-determination was beginning to replace imperial civilizing missions as the world's political ideology. The result of World War II sped that on, its aftermath generating considerable ethnic cleansing of minorities, but it reinforced secular tendencies already underway.

JAH: Didn't stop Hitler from trying to create an empire.

MM: No, nor the Japanese, but I think that what destroyed Hitler, fascism, and Japan alike was the militarism of their imperial projects, their overreliance on their own military prowess, regardless of the extent of their economic power. Their militarism induced recklessness in creating and taking on more and more enemies. A lower-level factor was that the Nazis and the Japanese behaved quite abominably in conquered areas that had often welcomed them in the first place. They generated counter-nationalisms as a result. There are faint echoes of this in the behavior of the United States today.

JAH: Just a quick digression here, before returning to China. Empires have collapsed over the ages for varied reasons. It sounds here as if you are arguing that this is true of modern empires—sometimes destroyed by nationalism but just as often by overextension. Is that a correct observation?

MM: Not really, though we must distinguish various types of empire here. The old colonial empires only proved to be overextended when they began to have some economic success during the twentieth century. This ironically created a new and disloyal middle class and trade unions, which when assisted by World War II sought more political powers. When that was resisted, they demanded and fought for full independence. It was only at that point that the colonial powers realized they lacked the power to keep on suppressing them, and the British and Dutch did cost–benefit analyses that made colonies seem not worthwhile. Not the French, however. They had to be beaten in battle to quit.

As for Germany and Japan, the new empires, their fall was distinctive, the last gasp of European militarism.

World War I begat popular paramilitary movements relying on the peculiar military combination of hierarchy and comradeship, which they believed could remake the world. That became fascism and it later launched World War II in both Europe and Asia— though I should add that in Japan "fascism" was not a mass movement but was largely confined to the officer corps. It did great damage there, however, greatly encouraging the Japanese assaults on China and then Pearl Harbor, and toward ultimate defeat. But what was quite unlike the collapse or decay of previous empires was the orderly, negotiated aftermath geopolitics. The allies first agreed what should be done, including the creation of the United Nations and Bretton Woods, and then each independent state joined this new world order and its new international organizations. The collapse of empires, except one, produced the new international order as well, and it was one that remained much more stable than the post-World War I aftermath.

JAH: But let us return to China. Do you think China is in some ways copying the United States? The country has a central ethnic core, albeit with some nationalist problems, but none so serious as to affect the possibility of becoming a nation-state. And it seeks to have secure sources of supply, possibly from Africa, and perhaps secure markets, too.

MM: In many ways Chinese power elites are adapting American practices. But if you are also implying that China might recreate that duality of nation-state at home, empire abroad, I doubt it. It is true that China, like Japan before it, feels the need for some kind of expansion in search of the raw materials that it lacks (or will soon lack) at home. But its expansion seems market-based, not territory- or military-based. It is also expanding mainly in Africa, where it doesn't immediately have to confront the United States. It's not imperialism: there's no coercion involved. Insofar as there is coercion of labor, it's with the agreement of the local government, as occurs in special enterprise zones throughout the world. China and the US are also highly economically interdependent, they both have nuclear weapons, and China has started modernizing its armed forces. The two know full well that they should avoid armed conflict with each other, or even indirect conflict through intermediaries, as was the Cold War custom. Tibet is a Hollywood issue and not a Washington one, and quite rightly, too. It would be very counterproductive for the US to offer any support for Tibetan autonomy. Taiwan might conceivably produce dangerous situations for them both, because of the unpredictable effects of Chinese and Taiwanese nationalisms, but not Africa.

JAH: The other sense of democracy that we have not yet talked about is that of liberal democracy. Perhaps the most successful article written in our times was that of Francis Fukuyama (1989), saying as the Cold War ended that "the world is now one," that there was no alternative to liberalism and capitalism. It doesn't quite look like that now. One sees now the emergence of authoritarian capitalist states, notably Russia but China is not totally dissimilar. Does that combination of authority plus capitalism seem stable to you? It's rather like Wilhelmine Germany. One can indeed ask whether Wilhelmine Germany would have lasted if not for defeat in World War I?

MM: There is some similarity. Wilhelmine Germany aimed at some social citizenship while restricting civil and political citizenship, as does China. But Germany was already semi-democratic in the liberal sense: the rule of law, parliament and parties and elections, were already there, coexisting with a semi-autonomous monarchy and bureaucracy. The social democratic party was already the largest single party, and there were going to be some more compromises made.

But that's a different question to what's happening now in the world. There is considerable uncertainty, but one thing that's been clear is that insofar as there is a relationship between level of development and liberal democracy, the level of development that's required has been going up steadily. India is the great exception; it was a very poor country when it institutionalized liberal democracy. Otherwise, decade through decade, you have had to be richer in order to transition to democracy. There are both waves toward and counter-waves away from democracy, as Samuel Huntington (1991) observed, and a counter-wave seems to be developing right now, specializing not in military regimes but in phony democracy: there are elections, but they are fixed; there are multiple parties, but the regime can choose their candidates and selectively ban them; and so on. The phenomenal economic success of China has certainly encouraged the notion that order must be prioritized over representation to achieve development. The expansion of democracy into the world remains considerably feebler and fraught with difficulties than is the expansion of capitalism. Since it is less capitalism that spreads democracy than resistance to capitalism, it is the conditions generating resistance that matter most.

Yet at the same time a state like China can't be just authoritarian because its stability depends on keeping the population reasonably content. The Chinese leaders are themselves aware now that they have to give more to their own people and that they have to engage in more infrastructure development and the like. There is even some officially sanctioned movement going on at the local level and in labor law, with trial local elections going on and workers feeling able to strike and develop unofficial unions. Most observers believe that is likely to increase, but any move to multi-party democracy would be fraught with difficulty and I doubt the regime will go that far in the foreseeable future.

JAH: So there is no necessary logic between rising incomes, greater technical skills, and demand for more rights which eventually turns into liberal democracy?

MM: Well, there is some relationship, but it's a much slower, less steady relationship than people thought. There are possibly bigger disruptions in the world that can easily throw this off.

JAH: Certainly, although it is also true that liberal democracy often comes on the back of great destructions.

MM: But liberal democracy is not always what it's cracked up to be. I think that the essence of genuine liberal democracy is pluralism, as Dahl (1989) and Lipset (1963) noted. Translated into my terms, pluralism becomes the separation of the four sources of power from each other. The problem of the Soviet Union was that all four sources of central power were fused in a single party elite, creating the absolute inverse of democracy. The United States obviously does not have that problem. It has securely subordinated military to civilian rule, it largely guarantees civil liberties, it has somewhat free elections, and there isn't a dominant ideology that might legitimate rule by a single group. But there is an increasing encroachment of economic power upon the political process itself. The cost of election campaigns and the extent of the financing of both parties by big business and powerful professions in return for favors have grown alarmingly. The tendency of Supreme Court decisions over the last 30 years has been especially worrying, for it has declared that a corporation should have the same rights as an individual, and thus its vast expenditures on elections and candidates are to be regarded as a form of free speech. That bizarre judgment reveals the extent to which capitalist ideology has captured American law and politics and reinforces the invasion of the political realm by economic power relations. The consequence is that it is very difficult to pass legislation that is against business interests, for example to reverse the astonishing recent growth of inequality within the United States or to develop a health care system that caters to the needs of its citizens. America is no longer the "City on the Hill," the shining beacon of pluralist democracy for the world. Any imperial mission needs cleaning up at home first. The corruption of Italian politics by the Berlusconi regime is another alarming example.

JAH: I would have thought that your own most critical comment about liberal democracy is of that of the very limited capacity it has to control foreign policy. International relations are still, as we saw in the case of the United States under the younger Bush, an astonishingly private affair. The records indicate not exactly a conspiracy, but key decisions being taken by a very small number of people.

MM: You're right. That is how the 2003 Iraq war was conducted. I think that is as close as normally rather messy states (in which the left hand often doesn't know what the right hand is doing) come to a conspiracy. Yes, the alarming thing about foreign policy is how it's still largely a private affair. Statesmen and stateswomen—no difference between them despite the optimistic views of some feminists—devise foreign policy and they do it with precious little relationship to the interests or views of the mass of the population.

Part of the problem is that the degree of nationalism among the population enables elites to commit us to war, and enables the war for a short period to be quite popular. The regime drapes itself in the flag and dissident voices are regarded as being suspect, unpatriotic, disloyal. The fundamental problem of foreign policy is that it is run by elites in private plus the lobbying of a few special interests who have a vested interest in the part of the world being decided upon. It's a failure of the nation-state.

JAH: Surely simply a failure of liberal democracy?

MM: Yes, but specifically the national vision, which is limited to the boundary of the state, inside of which you have strong interests and praxis concerning only domestic political issues.

JAH: So the national loyalty coming from engagement in war, or, rather, the popularity that comes from going into a war, is as present in an authoritarian nation-state as it can be, for a period at least, inside a liberal democratic one?

MM: Though perhaps liberal democratic states are quicker to deal with their lack of success, quicker to pull out.

JAH: Popular pressure played a part in getting out of Vietnam. But popular pressure is not nearly as present in the United States now.

MM: Well, it would be if there were equivalent losses to those in Vietnam. The US has taken great steps to minimize casualties—bombing from a safe height, the massive expansion in use of unmanned Predator drones, and the like—to reduce the publicity given to casualties, and to link them to the need for a War on Terror in very concrete ways—constant revelations of supposed terrorist plots in the US, security lines at airports and public buildings, and so on. The fact that its drones create more civilian casualties and thereby more terrorists is perversely used to demonstrate the greater threat confronting us rather than our own contribution to that threat. So the perception of failure now could be a longer-drawn-out process than it was in Vietnam.

JAH: When you were talking about liberal democracy needing to get its act together, you were, I think, really talking about the United States.

MM: Yes, particularly the United States, of which I am a citizen, and which remains easily the most important liberal democracy in the world while also degenerating from within.

JAH: I stressed that because a good deal of your recent work notes, in a very strong sense, the varied ways in which states can swim within capitalist society. You seem to regard the social citizenship—social democratic in Scandinavia, Christian democratic in Germany and Italy—as well established.

MM: In the course of writing Volume III one thing that was firmed up for me was my preference for contemporary regimes that have a strong measure of social citizenship coming in social democratic and Christian democrat forms. The predominant one in Continental Europe is the postwar economic compromise that was effectively made between capital and labor, and the political compromise that was made between social democracy and Christian democracy, for fear of a return of either fascism or communism. That was one of the silver linings of the extremely dark cloud which was World War II.

JAH: So you've become deeply conservative of those achievements of the most attractive political form that has
been created in the modern world. Maintaining those
achievements clearly matters to you a great deal in
prescriptive terms.

MM: The Europeans can be congratulated on their achievements in the second half of the twentieth century, in
great contrast to their appalling failures in the first half
of the century. And I hope very much that they can
retain these achievements under current pressures.
Luckily for them, they managed to entrench those
citizen rights in corporatist institutions within their
states, and these are difficult to shift. From the 1970s
on there has been a growing conservative movement
developing across advanced capitalist countries, always
taking a pro-capital, anti-labor form and often a neoliberal form. In the face of this the social/Christian
democracy compromise has clearly stalled—no more
progressive reforms—but so far has not been forced
to retreat much. In contrast neoliberalism has swept
away the more voluntarist mixed liberal–labor version
of this, which was dominant in the Anglophone
countries.

The fundamental reasons for these shifts derived from
the end of the "golden age of capitalism" during which
gains had been made out of growth. But in the 1970s
as recession hit and profit rates shriveled, the class
struggle became zero-sum, and it was much more difficult for leftists to continue making gains, and in fact
they didn't. At best they have preserved what they had
because of being entrenched inside the state. In Scandinavia and much of continental Europe the corporatist state locks its various clients into existing power
relations more effectively than happens in more liberal
countries like the US, Britain, Australia, New Zealand,

and Ireland. This, their own form of "conservatism," has been to preserve a larger measure of social citizenship, whereas there has been a substantial regression in liberal countries. Some of the problems of the United States have spread to the other Anglo countries. If you think about it in terms of levels of inequality, for example, the United States is now extreme among the OECD countries, but Britain, Australia, and New Zealand are not far behind. But these comparisons also show that there is no single best way of running a capitalist economy. On most indices Scandinavian and continental European countries do equally well as or even better than the Anglophones on economic growth, and they do better on more social indicators such as life expectancy, infant mortality, or hours worked. There are alternatives.

This also raises broader political and ideological issues. While writing Volume III I became more aware of what might be called the "macro-regional" influences from the neighbors and cultural kin of individual nation-states. In this sense the individual nation-states are less insulated, or maybe this was just something I didn't notice in the past. I've been impressed by the way in which macro-regions influence welfare regimes and varieties of capitalism. The Anglophones, Nordics, Continental Europeans (with Mediterranean countries separating somewhat from their northern neighbors in recent years), Latin Americans, East Asians—and there may be more, too—manifesting distinctive trajectories of development. These groups have real commonalities in the way that they develop capitalism, the way that they develop welfare regimes, and what they think of as the natural way of doing things. Most of them are formed by a neighborhood culture, though Anglophone culture is dispersed through countries all over the world, related by kin, language, and shared histories.

It is very important that in this period leadership shifted from one Anglophone country to another, making it extremely unlikely that there would be major conflict occurring with this transformation, which was obviously not the case when Germany strove for hegemony. Even today we can see that it is essentially only the Anglophone nations among the more advanced countries that can be defined as being relatively neoliberal, having developed not just a fairly unregulated financial sector, which is common across most of the world, but also having significantly cut back welfare, reduced labor union power, and become most unequal. The common contrast is between the nation-state and global and transnational institutions, yet we often see institutions at this in-between macro-regional level.

JAH: So actually you're going a little bit beyond the "varieties of capitalism" based on a rather simple binary contrast between neoliberal and state-dominated forms of capitalism. You're saying there are several types, including those practiced in East Asia and Latin America.

MM: When one extends analysis over more of the world one sees the essential kinship of the Latin American countries. For a very long time they were the most unequal countries of the world, since ethnic-racial differences of conquest and slavery were superimposed on class relations and land reform has never happened. They certainly are highly unequal today, although they are being rivaled by the growing inequality of the United States and some of the former Soviet Bloc countries. East Asia is a distinct "developmental" type, well-known in the literature, and it remains so even after having to make adaptations to international financial institutions operating under the Washington neoliberal consensus. Though one mustn't push these things too far; one mustn't be either too nation-statist or too globalist either. So in this region there are family resemblances among Japan, South Korea, Taiwan, and Singapore, and increasingly, as development also occurs, among Malaysia, the Philippines, Indonesia as well.

JAH: There might yet be some impact of China as a developmental model on places like Vietnam. So it's not to say that future models are to be ruled out.

MM: No, absolutely not. If China carries on being successful, others will seek to adapt its practices to their own. We should remember also that these different kinds of regime have distinct trajectories. They possess some flexibility and their differences from each other do not remain static. So if one took 1950, the Anglophone countries would be as equal as the Nordic countries. It was only in the 1960s that the Nordic countries became more equal, and it was only in the 1970s and 1980s that most of the continental European countries became more equal than the Anglos. Moreover, the detachment of the Mediterranean countries from the euro bloc seems to be growing as we speak. The great contrast between Latin America and East Asia, despite both containing "middle-class" countries, is their different histories of conquest, war, and land reform. Whereas Latin American conquest and the consequent land appropriation has not been challenged (at least until the last few years) and has never been disrupted by major war, East Asia saw very significant land reform as a consequence of the collapse of the European and Japanese empires in war. So we as analysts must be responsive to the specific changes that occur in all the sources of social power.

JAH: One last question about the United States. Although "the melting pot" still works, at least in my view, it remains just as crucial, if one wants to understand the political economy of welfare in that country, to remember the importance of race. Are not the limitations of social citizenship in the United States best explained by the refusal to extend all sorts of rights to African Americans? The work of Alberto Alesina shows that those states inside the United States that have smaller numbers of African Americans tend to have more generous welfare regimes than those that have more. Social citizenship in the United States is, surely, rather limited.

MM: It doesn't have *much* social citizenship. The fundamental precondition of social citizenship is that the working class and the lower middle class think of themselves as the same kind of people, and they have a degree of empathy and sympathy for each other such that they can imagine themselves being in the same position as others. Welfare states were essentially built on that solidarity, which extended and diffused the notion of being "working class" to a populist sense of the people as a whole, and even to the "nation," which was clear in the Swedish conception of a welfare state being a "people's home" or the current French description of it as *la solidarité nationale*. The New Deal in America and World War II in Britain were transforming moments in this direction, too. In the case of some continental European countries, it has involved a compromise between class differences and with religion, so that welfare is universal but not intrinsically very redistributive. Benefits differ by social statuses. They are universal benefit systems yet distributed through status differences.

Some very general threats have emerged to that solidarity. A general one is the rise in prosperity, meaning greater dispersion of incomes and workers moving into higher tax brackets, followed by recession, which tends to hurt ordinary people. Thoughts of "I will not be better off if I sympathize with the poor," and images of the "worthless poor" flourish. But the US has had more of this. Once African Americans achieved civil rights and became part of the citizen body rather than being a segregated, separated group, whites' racialism shifted into matters of welfare. Stereotypes of the poor as being black and possessing disabling cultures have played a substantial role in weakening white commitment to the New Deal legacy. That became clearly visible in the collapse of Johnson's Great Society program. Reagan was then able to attract large numbers of white workers away from liberalism and the Democratic Party. The conservative momentum of the last forty years owes much to the association of welfare with race. There is a lesser European equivalent of that now in immigration, whose tensions pose the greatest threat to the universal welfare state and to social citizenship.

JAH: You have been talking about class, putting ethnicity and race to one side. Might that not be wrong? Societies that are nationally homogeneous are likely to have generous welfare rights because sharing with people like yourself in ethnic or national terms is rather easy. A formerly totally homogeneous country such as Denmark, blessed hitherto with exceptionally generous welfare rights, is suddenly having difficulty in the face of immigration. At present it is managing to maintain social democracy for "real" Danes, but it is also finding a way to keep the immigrants out, or limited in number, in a form of national socialism. So isn't the variable ethnicity or race, as much as class?

MM: I wouldn't disagree with that. What I was trying to say about the United States was meant to indicate that race trumps class, and has consistently done so. Of course, it is coded. Politicians can't express any overt racism and haven't been able to do so for decades.

Racism is coded in concerns about crime, housing, and "welfare queens."

JAH: So it's an astonishing thing that advanced societies, the United States now and Hitler's Germany earlier, can be turned around and obsessed with a minority, which is, in effect, tiny.

MM: Yes, though these two cases are very different. There are more African Americans as a proportion of the population than there were Jews in Germany—12 percent compared to 0.8 percent. It is much more difficult to figure out why so many Germans could be brought to blame the Jews. For many white American workers there is a threat, or at least this seems highly plausible to them. We must conclude that they don't view themselves as the same kind of person as African Americans, or indeed as Mexican immigrants. The same is increasingly true of many native-born people in a number of European countries in relation to immigrants from Africa or Eastern Europe. Leftists have always criticized the New Deal for its limitations, especially its two-tier system of benefits, which has been both gendered and racialized. That was not traditionally true of most European welfare states, but potentially some regress toward the US system might occur in Europe. Just when Europe has achieved an enviable level of shared citizenship, new threats emerge to that.

4

An End to Ideology?

JAH: You have spoken in warm terms about the achievement of varied types of social citizenship in Europe. To what extent do these achievements represent a powerful ideology? One might argue that the achievements of liberal capitalism are not particularly ideological. "Consumers of the world, unite" is less morally striking than "Workers of the world, unite." Performative power is hardly a moral project. Are ideological projects less present now than they were in the recent historical record? In other words, is there an end to ideology?

MM: No, but obviously there is a contrast between the first half of the twentieth century and the second half up to today. Western countries are generally less ideological. They have buried fascism and communism. Social democracy is less ideological because it has some of the characteristics that you were attributing to liberal capitalism: it's more pragmatic. It's abandoned the notion that there is an alternative to capitalism. Instead, it assumes it can ameliorate capitalism and domesticate it . . . civilize it, give it a human face. It is largely what I call an institutionalized ideology plus some limited commitment to change.

JAH: So it's socialized democratic capitalism rather than democratic socialism?

MM: Not any longer. And nationalism, too, has been domesticated. The kind of nationalism that we have, for the most part in the advanced countries, with the exception of the immigration issue, is rather nice and harmless and sometimes quite funny, the delusions that each country has about its unique virtue and contribution to the world and the chants and costumes of its football supporters. Nationalism has changed considerably.

There remain smaller groups spouting leftist ideologies, some traditional, like socialism or anarchism, others new, like radical ecology. And on the other side, there are important conservative varieties of ideology in Western countries. In the US religious fundamentalism has had one of its periodic bursts into politics, while neoliberalism is a genuinely utopian ideology. It's like socialism, in a way. It doesn't describe a real society. A purely market society cannot be achieved and if they want to achieve any of their goals neoliberals have to rely on alliances with conservative politicians who supplement neoliberal programs with their own interests and ideals, like harsh punishment for criminals, racism, and a big military. In the past socialism was also compromised by political deal-making.

It's curious that American commentators on politics talk about the polarization of politics into two ideological camps, but actually there's one camp, the overwhelmingly cohesive Republican Party, blending neoliberalism with traditional American conservatism (militarism, moral values, racism now coded, and so on), while the Democrats are far more diverse. Growing conservative cohesion has characterized the last 40 or so years.

JAH: In the United States it's not just neoliberal ideas among elites that matter! It's also a moral majority, perhaps especially among Southern Baptists, often supporters of Israel. It's a rather diverse, sometimes even contradictory conservative ideology. But I accept that it is very powerful.

MM: Religious conservatism is regionally a powerful ideology. The practice of the Republican Party is obviously a compromise between diverse groups, but all are allowed to vent their ideological rhetoric and they do have certain common thrusts—against statism for example. That Obama's puny little health program could be rejected as "socialism" means there's a powerful ideology at work there.

JAH: In terms of ideology, do you see a big distinction between the advanced world and the rest of the world? When communism ended in Central Europe it was very noticeable that there was no ideology beyond wanting to get back to Europe. A huge historic change bred no new ideas. Are there other places in the world where ideology, however, does have real power?

MM: I think I would qualify what you say by noting great variations among countries. You are generally right about the European rim of the Soviet bloc. It did not need a utopia because it believed a much better society existed next door in the European Union. But in Russia itself neoliberalism was quite important and the connection between liberal democracy and a free market, especially as emphasized by neoliberalism, was quite important as an ideal. This provided a principled opposition to the pragmatic post-communism of people like Gorbachev and this played an important role in his downfall. We also see new ideology in the Muslim world, after the failure of Arab socialism and military regimes. There was another attempt to create some form of developmental ideology, an Islamist one, though I suspect it is already faltering (as it is in Iran), though American aggression is helping to boost its appeal. Conservative America has also strengthened its ideology. On the other hand, China does not have an ideological commitment anymore. There is much variation around the world—as was normal in less global eras.

JAH: The Chinese worship economic growth. That is a long way away from Bolshevism and Nazism, both of which had a moral theory *plus* the possibility of development. They provided total ideological packages. It doesn't seem as if anything quite like that exists in the world today.

MM: No, but there are other growing ideologies, such as environmentalism, feminism, and other identity politics.

JAH: Theorists sometimes see these as general ideologies, but don't you think they are more single-issue concerns?

MM: Some are, but feminism is rather a major single issue, while environmentalism is not a single issue but a worldview with a very general moral view of the human relationship to nature. Many environmentalists also claim that their form of activism produces a more vibrant democracy. There has been a decline of ideology since the first half of the twentieth century, and a good thing, too! But ideologies are not finished. They re-emerge with each crisis that does not appear to be solvable from within existing institutionalized ideologies, and then people seek new general meaning systems. For good or ill, the coming environmental crisis will likely do just this.

JAH: You once noted that Max Weber recognized different sources of social power, but said that there was little pattern to their relations—at any time one of them might be dominant. At various times in your work you have made claims as to when and why one form of power was dominant. Ideology had enormous power when it created world religions, thereby changing the shape of history, while political and economic power rather than ideology mattered in the long nineteenth century. Have you revised your viewpoint? Were you surprised to begin to discover that the twentieth century was so ideological?

MM: Let's leave until later the more general issue of the relations between the power sources. But on ideology I did not get it quite right in Volume II. What I wrote there about the decline in ideology was much more about religion in Europe than anything else. I still see it as Eurocentrically true, but it isn't true in many other places. Was I surprised by the revival of ideology in the twentieth century? No, because I worked on fascism in the meantime, but clearly it was a discontinuity from the nineteenth century. Though socialist movements were already growing then, World War I and the Great Depression were required for the tremendous surge of ideology, of almost utopian ways of reorganizing society after the disasters brought upon it.

JAH: Surely, heroic ideology was present in Russia, at least among its intellectuals, before World War I?

MM: Ideologies were present among the intellectuals, and notably in France as well as Russia, but not as a mass mobilizing force. That was especially true of fascism, though socialism was partly an exception since it was already big in prewar Germany. But it is likely that without war any attempt at a leftist revolution would have been repressed rather than being successful. It was the mobilization of the armed forces that really allowed revolutions to take place after World War I, though even then only one was successful, in Russia.

In general, the problem of the twentieth century, and a theme of my third volume, is that it's ridden by a number of great crises, which bring some very unexpected events and processes while also reinforcing or diminishing others. We can't quite see in the future what equivalent tendencies might be. For example we don't know how the rise of China and India will continue, whether they will experience or introduce major crises. We don't know what the consequences will be of major environmental crises, principally because it is unclear whether human beings can mitigate them before the worst happens. But such crises could well be the equivalent of what happened in the twentieth century, generating major dislocations and new ideologies, as the old ways don't work and a group of intellectuals and the others emerge with some blueprint for the future, which has a degree of plausibility and can mobilize enough people to cause disruption and even to launch coups, revolutions, and wars.

JAH: That's to say that something like that could happen again, given that the future is indeterminate.

5

Patterns, Cages, Interstices, and a Dialectic

JAH: Your work on power does not just concern the four sources we have identified. Rather, there are a series of middle-range theories, less well known but to my mind of great fertility. I'd like to take some of them in turn. At present you seem to see a certain predominance of economic power with some interruptions from military events, both in combination with the presence of the nation-state ideal.

MM: There is an underlying continuity with the nineteenth century in the sense that there is a dual causal process in overall social development. On the one hand, capitalism and its classes, or I should say economic modes of production and classes, because we have had to deal with state socialism in the twentieth century, which had its own economic structures and stratifications; and on the other hand, the development of the political powers of the nation-state in an initially imperial world. The general development of the twentieth century is the victory of a more socialized capitalism as the solvent of class struggle, and an imperial United States as the solution to inter-imperial strife yet remaining in tension with a developing nation-state system.

It is unclear whether China continues to represent a challenge to capitalism, for there is no term that accurately describes the Chinese mode of production. I don't think it is quite capitalist because the state plays too important a role, and enterprises are often run solely or jointly by local or central state officials. It's obviously not remotely socialist anymore but a quite distinct form. But apart from that, capitalism is the economic system of the world, and whether it brings development or not is perhaps the most important issue for the individual nation-states.

So through the vicissitudes of military and ideological power through the twentieth century—and they have been considerable—there is nonetheless some continuity, though at an increasingly global level, of the economic predominance of capitalism, and a dual political predominance of the nation-state and American Empire. But there is no single form of either capitalism or the nation-state, and there is uncertainty about what will succeed American Empire.

The complication here, however, is globalization. Most early theorists of globalization believed it was essentially transnational, undermining nation-states. Though there are transnational processes underway, especially in the capitalist economy, the main political principle of globalization has been international, regulation by and competition between states—relations of geopolitical and geo-economic power, not transnational relations. When capitalists seek aid or regulation, they turn to the state. Most global issues are negotiated between states, especially the more powerful states. And because of the increasing irrationality of war, brought about by nuclear and other weapons, "soft" geopolitics are intensifying much more than "hard geopolitics." These will continue to intensify. It is through soft geopolitics that climate change, probably the major crisis of the next half-century, should be confronted.

JAH: Let us turn to your notion of "caging," that is, the capacity of states to capture social actors. Is it the case that caging is weakening now for two particular types of actors? First of all, capitalists seem at times foot-loose and fancy-free, thereby gaining a certain amount of leverage inside societies. Second, some of the elites of the developing world want to be part of global society, and seem prepared accordingly to abandon their nations to their own fate.

MM: I think that some have experienced a decline of national caging. Capitalists, especially finance capitalists, have a greater degree of autonomy and mobility potential. This is less true for manufacturing. Though much of it has relocated to low-wage countries, its headquarters are mostly located in its home country and its profits are repatriated there (or to offshore tax havens). Practitioners of some professions, including academics like us, are also much more transnational than was so in the recent past. But most migration is of lower-skilled people and that tends to result more in a bina-tional way of life than a transnational one.

In the economic realm there was a period of national Keynesianism, national development programs, import substitution industrialization and the like, and that has declined somewhat in the face of global pressures and neoliberalism, but the power of the latter varies con-siderably across the world and has been recently revealing its frailties. Various compromises are emerg-ing. Many developing countries have recently resisted finance capital by building up reserves of their own. Others have formally adhered to neoliberal prescrip-tions but their practices on the ground largely continue as before. Neoliberals themselves complain perpetually that their programs are undermined by national power interests and political corruption. WTO free trade talks have now been stalled for a decade, while some limited degree of financial reregulation is now occurring. Capitalism is still nationally demarcated. There are still significant national boundaries. This is less true of capitalism in Europe, of course, but Europe is exceptional and in any case its nation-states still flourish within the EU.

JAH: But the power of capitalism to move—finance for sure, but at least sometimes manufacturing—can kick back quite significantly on national societies. In the German case, taking full advantage of cheap labor in post-communist countries does seem to have some relationship to the declining wages of German manual workers.

MM: That also happens in the United States, at the lower end, yes.

JAH: And what about the elites of developing societies?

MM: There were probably more native collaborators with imperialism in its heyday, while merchants trading internationally were often of different ethnicities from the local population among whom they operated. Both groups are still active. Local entrepreneurs collaborating with foreign capital have presumably increased in numbers, as has the fifth column of local neoliberal economists trained in the United States.

JAH: A third "middle range" insight into power that has structured your thought in the past has been the importance of the emergence of interstitial power sources. Does this concept help us understand our world?

MM: Well, insofar as developments being unexpected, emerging from the interstices of previous social structures, that remains important. The environmental issue is a spectacular example, since it is the consequence of everything that we've regarded as constituting economic success in the nineteenth and twentieth centuries. The more successful you are in economic development, the more problematic the aftermath, generating new problems for human societies to solve. What are generally called the "new social movements"—environmentalism, feminism, and other recent identity politics movements—are examples of interstitial emergence. The discourse of individual rights emerged out of the originally class-based struggles for full citizenship, and it has become a major success story of this period. Feminism is an example of a movement that emerges interstitially and largely succeeds in its goals, country by country, and in the process becomes gradually institutionalized, in this case at both the national and the international (for example, the United Nations) level. Gay and disability rights are similarly diffusing.

JAH: I accept what you say about environmentalism, to which we turn at length later. What about the emergence of international terrorists, al-Qaeda above all?

MM: That's another unanticipated emergence in which tiny numbers of people, though with a much larger body of sympathizers, have unexpectedly emerged to create consequential threats out of all proportion to their numbers and previously supposed powers. They, together with hawks in Washington and London, have created a "War on Terror" which is affecting all our lives.

JAH: So it is small, whereas science plus environmentalism might actually be much more significant?

MM: Terrorists are significant, though victory over them is potentially achievable. Tough international police operations combined with non-interventionism in Muslim lands would probably slow and then halt the flow of new terrorist recruits. But the environmental issues are much more difficult to solve, and they have already generated a very large social movement operating at two different levels, the community of scientists and popular green activism. The scientists are already within government as established advisors in all kinds of relevant institutions, while the NGOs have a more popular mobilizing and disturbing force. The combination has had quite a rapid growth, even though there's a long way to go before decisive influence is exerted on governments and corporations.

JAH: So mass movements like the one we saw in Seattle in 1999?

MM: They combine environmentalism with broader anti-capitalist ideology and politics. Their range is very broad. The environmental movements range from anarchists and eco-terrorists through to extremely respectable, old established environmental protection movements such as the Sierra Club or Royal Societies for the Protection of anything, with organizations like Greenpeace operating somewhere in between. Their combined rhetoric has influence. Political parties in Europe are now competing at least rhetorically in claims to be the "Green" party. There aren't many important Green-titled parties, but the established parties have moved quite rapidly in a number of countries to make claims in this area, which is really quite interesting. It is an attempt at institutionalization that most movements are resisting because the parties do not go nearly far enough in actually implementing any policies.

JAH: The final issue I wish to raise concerns the dialectic with which you ended the first volume of *The Sources of Social Power*. Looking back at the *longue durée* of human history, you noted a dialectic—a continual interaction—between centralizing power and decentralizing societal responses. Tools that were originally deployed by central power, such as literacy, went out into society and soon proved useful as means of defense against the state. It was a good idea, but you haven't used it much since. Is it relevant now?

MM: It is still relevant, though in changing forms. Actually, two contrasts were involved, the state–society dialectic to which you refer and the dialectic between domination between centralized empires and what I called multi-power actor civilizations—in the ancient Mediterranean contrasting the Assyrian or Roman empires with the Greek or Phoenician city-states. In the twentieth century the latter dialectic is revealed in the contrast between empire and nation-state and between state socialism and fascism on the one hand and democratic capitalism on the other—relatively centralized versus relatively decentralized. Of course, the solution to their conflict was more complex and more pragmatic. Fascism was actually overthrown by the greater centralized, mobilized military power wielded by the unholy alliance between communism and democratic capitalism. While state socialism always faced an uphill battle not only against capitalism's superior ability to innovate and its decentralized powers, but also against the superior centralized power of its core, the American Empire. The process and the victory have been more complex than the stark contrasts might suggest.

Moreover, the process of globalization has filled the world, so there is no longer the space at the margins for the successors to occupy first. The historical form of the dialectic, where the opposite model appears first in the interstices or on the margins of the previously dominant one, may be at an end. Conceptual schemes always apply better in some times and places than others—that is the problem of the messiness of human societies and of their historical development, both of which lead to totally new social crises requiring new sociological concepts. At the most general level I would claim that my model of the sources of social power is sufficiently light and open—a cloak lightly thrown over the shoulders rather than an iron cage—to be helpful across space and time. But tighter models like dialectics are better in some contexts than others.

JAH: I wonder if it might not have more mileage to it than you suggest. The internet was more or less developed inside a centralized state for its own purposes, but the new capacities of communication that it brings can certainly curtail central power. Are there going to be any long-term consequences to diffusion of new technical tools?

MM: That is an example of the first dialectic still operating. The internet has added to the organizing powers of these international movements, these supposedly transnational NGOs. The internet is perhaps the most transnational element of their organization because NGOs themselves tend to be international federations of national movements, but the internet clearly has enabled a degree of organization from the bottom up—even though most NGOs do not have democratic constitutions. They certainly go down to the middle-class level, which is far more populist than political establishments, and that is something that is significant. But feminism is a good example of a movement operating at three levels: organizing simultaneously at the national government level, which is necessary to actually pass feminist legislation; at the international UN level, which can pressure governments to conform to international norms; and at the transnational level through the internet. The movement managed to persuade many governments of the South, including some rather reactionary ones, that educating women was an important way to reduce population growth, which is one of their main problems. So that is something where it's had an impact, both through the highest levels of international organization like the UN, but also through better transnational communication among activists.

But regimes also use the internet, often against the NGOs. They monitor and hack it, learning of oppositional tactics and timetables. At the G8, G20 and other international meetings, the anarchists and other leftist groups have learned not to use either the internet or cellphones, since their movements can be more easily tracked there. So I am not so sure that the internet is all that important in changing power relations.

JAH: The Orange Revolution, even if it seems to have failed, was certainly influenced by these techniques.

MM: But it was aided by considerable American subsidies. And don't forget that the Orange Revolution didn't actually accomplish much, since the reality of the Ukraine is that the country is split almost exactly in two by the Russian–Ukrainian divide. Democracy again turned into an ethnic plebiscite.

JAH: Then there are simpler means of communication. I was once in Indonesia and felt at the start that Islam there was very different from that of the Middle East. But visiting medrasahs, the religious schools, partly changed my mind: for the first time in Indonesia access was possible to Wahabi texts, which were clearly in use in that country, creating what was truly a new set of societal responses.

Part Two

The Nature of Social Change

6

States, Strong and Weak

JAH: I'd like to begin a discussion of states as agents of change by talking about Great Britain. For a short period it was a leader of world power, so a discussion of its fate will help raise questions about the contemporary world—in which a new leading power is facing challenges that some hold to be similar to those of its Anglo-Saxon predecessor.

Does your long essay on "The Decline of Great Britain" seem dated now? Britain in the Blair years looked economically more powerful, even though it is suffering again. Do you think Britain was knocked off its perch?

MM: Britain was permanently knocked off its Great Power perch, which had been an extraordinary achievement for such a small country. It had been based on a period-specific naval-commercial empire which had managed to found major white settler colonies and capture India, the whole being reinforced by its invention of the Industrial Revolution. When that revolution spread and other countries developed great powers and pretensions, Britain's role in the front rank was bound to be over.

There has been a bit of a recovery of sorts initiated by Thatcher and Blair, but geopolitically it has made Britain more dependent on the United States than it used to be. There's been something of an economic revival, but along its traditional lines of finance more than industry, and this has very recently made for greater instability. Militarily and geopolitically Britain is the equal of France but with less autonomy. In terms of economic power Britain is somewhere behind Germany and Japan, but in the top tier of the next group of Western countries. It punches less than its weight in the European Union, but its currency is one of the lesser internationally traded ones. So decline has not continued but Britain has settled down into a lesser role.

JAH: I agree completely with the geopolitical point you have just made. But what about the critique insisting that the economy suffered because finance capitalism mattered more than its industrial counterpart? Surely the relative recovery goes against your initial diagnosis?

MM: No. Along with greater financial power has come greater instability and vulnerability. Britain has suffered more than France or Germany in the current great recession. There is also a significant widening of inequality within Britain. Whatever the overall GDP figures, it is more maldistributed than it used to be, and more people have effectively lost much of their social citizenship and do not participate in the economy to the extent that they would like. Britain has the same kind of unemployment problem as the United States. Its formal level of unemployment is about 8 percent plus much more casual and part-time employment than in most of Europe. It's a recovery for some only.

JAH: It's recovery in a period when finance capitalism was very important, which could use the skills of the City of London. But if finance capital changed in some way, for example by relocating, the British position might not be at all strong.

MM: Well, British governments continue to protect the City of London and they are unlikely to agree to any re-regulation of the international financial sector which might downsize the City, and there it has a powerful ally in the United States. So I wouldn't expect to see very much change, just a little bit of tightening. Clearly in the long run, as American power declines relatively and more growth is occurring in Asia, that will affect the City of London, and British economic power may further decline a little.

JAH: The amount of attention that you have devoted to the United States in recent years, seen as the leading edge of power in recent history, is very striking—so we must consider its position a little more, even at the risk of repetition. When writing about the decline of Great Britain, you noted three processes that could lead to a leading power losing its position: diffusion of techniques to the larger capitalist society; the institutionalization of its moment of success, such that it found it hard to adopt new ideas and techniques; and, geopolitically, being knocked off its perch. Well nobody has knocked the United States off its perch, geopolitically, and I find it hard to see this happening. I would also reiterate the hidden strength of the United States in economic terms, not least in terms of the institutions that support technological innovation. Twenty years ago it seemed as though Japan was going to be "number one," but it doesn't look like that now. Then there is the question of institutionalizing a moment of success. Surely the United States is not suffering too badly in terms of the factors you identified? It's not going to be anything like a sudden decline; it might be able to maintain its position for really a very long time.

MM: That is right. The period of American dominance
came in stages. The United States became the biggest
economy by the beginning of the twentieth century.
The main home of the second Industrial Revolution
was the United States, followed closely by Germany
and then Britain. The rest of the twentieth century has
essentially seen the working-out of the technologies
that were developed in that period, and there hasn't
been a comparable revolution in technology since then
that had such a big effect on the economy. Whereas a
general-purpose technology like electricity enabled
mass production and generated all kinds of inventions
in terms of iron, steel, chemicals, and so on, as well
as revolutionizing agriculture, the inventions that have
happened in the postwar period have not had such
radical effects. We tend to be very impressed by com-
puters and biotechnology but they have not led to
anywhere near comparable growth.

Second, however, it was World War II that greatly and
suddenly enhanced American power. America had
contributed about 15 percent of world GDP in the late
1930s, but in 1950 it had half the world's GDP, an
accident of war—more precisely of victory in war with
very little sacrifice by itself and no destruction at all
to its home territory. Third, when people say that the
United States has a minimal social welfare system, they
tend not to count education, and here the United States
has always been among the leading group of countries.
In the nineteenth century it led in elementary education, in the first half of the twentieth century in sec-
ondary education, and then after World War II, Korea,
and the Sputnik launch it developed its unparalleled
university sector, and that obviously has very close
links to its capacities in R & D. So we're still in the
period of American economic—and of course
military—dominance.

JAH: And it's likely to continue, given that the application of science to industrial life, so prominent in the United States, will be important in the future.

MM: But not uniquely and it is not now leading in the development of new technologies to combat climate change. This is an area in which China is also making major development, as well as Germany and other European countries. The main previous technological advantage of the US was the ability to cheaply and extensively exploit its natural resources. Today the US emits more greenhouse gases per capita of the population than any other country. We now see this as extremely wasteful and environmentally dangerous. Faced with environmental problems, the US has to shift gears more than any other advanced country, a difficult task.

JAH: The British Empire only really lasted as long as there was a balance of power in Europe, allowing it to predominate elsewhere. At the moment the United States does not face a challenge equivalent to that which Germany presented to Great Britain.

MM: No, there are no geopolitical challengers. The only scenario that one could envisage is the challenge presented by the end of the dollar as the single reserve currency in the world. That would mean that the Americans would have to pay more for their military, and that would give them pause. China might also be a rival, with its own sphere of influence over Asia and perhaps Africa, too. So we would no longer have the unique period of single-power dominance over the world.

JAH: What about the third element of your analysis, institutionalizing a moment of success? I have the impression when you write about America these days that you note a very static, trapped society unable to get out of certain patterns. Is that correct?

MM: That generalization works quite well for the US. At the moment it seems true ideologically and politically. Ideologically, Americans continue to view their country as the greatest in the world, bringing order to the world, but this is now becoming less true. Similarly, the anti-statism and neoliberalism endemic in America will hinder adjustment to economic and environmental problems. It seems to particularly damage the Republican Party, which is in a sorry state. In politics the separation of powers has become the stalemating of power.

The development of the Republican Party has been toward becoming an ideologically cohesive party, rejecting any notion of change and becoming more anti-statist, "little American," and even anti-science. The anti-statism is a very good example of increasingly institutionalizing those conditions that are thought to have made America great in the past. This is not so marked among the Democrats, but their relative diversity makes them less reform-oriented than they used to be, since a quarter or a third of them, the "blue dogs" and "black dogs," fearing increasing conservatism or dependent on conservative industries like oil or coal, will no longer support reform. The electorate is divided, and changes in the committee structure on the Hill mean that the parties, and not seniority, decide who will chair Congressional committees; while the filibuster rules have been increasingly interpreted in a very broad sense. In the past, the filibuster was only used for major issues that representatives felt very strongly about, like Southerners and desegregation / states' rights. Now the filibuster is threatened on almost everything. The result is near-deadlock, or legislation whose sometimes sweeping intent is almost completely undermined by the fine print resulting from endless compromises.

The exception, and the only significant area of power autonomy, is that of the Presidency in foreign policy, which has increased through the twentieth century and has increased again recently because of the backing up of that Presidential authority with the War on Terror and its surveillance/security apparatuses. The result is that the President can get the country into war or peace, for good or ill. Yet unfortunately any international treaty—and that is increasingly the way global issues are resolved—is extraordinarily difficult to get through Congress. The US is not well-placed at the moment to resist its future decline.

JAH: Let us now turn to other countries so as to see the extent to which they are active on the world stage. In the last seven or eight years there has been a great deal of discussion about the BRICs, and I'd like you to comment on each of them. They seem to have very different levels of potential power. So let's begin with Russia: is it really going to be a member of a group capable of challenging the United States?

MM: But perhaps the first question is whether these countries in fact form a collective group. Not really, except in size and rate of growth of GDP. They rarely act collectively and they are rather diverse. There are still territorial disputes between China and Russia, and between China and India, while Brazil is very different from the rest. India and China have much stronger economies than the others. Russia is a much weaker economy; very resource-dependent, not yet fully recovered from the disastrous transition from what had become a disastrous form of state socialism. Two are democracies, one is rather mixed (Russia), one remains authoritarian (China). Russia, China, and India have significant armed forces, but Brazil does not.

JAH: Russia is buying ships from France that they can no longer make themselves; that suggests catastrophic decline. Of course, the transition is disastrous in terms of living standards and mortality rates, but historically for a Great Power to collapse with such a small amount of violence is a remarkable success.

MM: Provided it leads to something better. It was quite extraordinary and unprecedented. It fell from the top; it fell from the collapse of the cohesion of the Communist Party, the loss of belief in the socialism they were supposed to be pursuing. The Party had become a set of bureaucratic apparatuses incapable of reform or of generating a political debate about reform. Thus the Gorbachev reformers couldn't devise a coherent plan. Of course, in quasi-revolutionary situations people stumble their way to a new form of regime, but in this case they failed, and a failed military coup then finished them off, succeeded by failed neoliberalism. Then leading politicians realized that neoliberalism couldn't be implemented without mass popular unrest, and so they cut it back and we had a series of confused policies and gradual recovery back to where they had been before but with an even greater dependence on natural and energy resources than before. Russia is exercising power within its own regional sphere of influence, but is in no shape to help lead a global restructuring project.

JAH: There's a big contrast to be drawn, I think, between Central Europe, living in this system for forty years, able to recover a certain view of its place in the West, blessed even with elements of institutional continuity, and Russia, the home of the first absolutely failed social revolution. Sometimes you get the impression of complete confusion in the Russian case.

In contrast you have been impressed by the Chinese Communist Party's ability both to make a revolution, and to continue to so reform itself as to be able to participate effectively in the modern world. What is the secret of that reform?

MM: The obvious overriding policy, reinforced by the Russian experience, is to go for economic reform without political reform, to maintain the leading role of the Party, that is, the authoritarian state.

JAH: *Perestroika* before *glasnost*?

MM: China is *perestroika* without *glasnost*. Through the decades of its economic reform program, when things went wrong in the experiments they were currently undertaking, the Central Committee of the Party would say, "Okay, we will stop that," and change to another path. That central power remained, and remained capable of determining what was successful and what was not. But I think that there are subsidiary points as well. On the other hand, the Chinese Communist Party was always more decentralized than its Soviet counterpart because of the way the revolutions happened. In China it was made by diverse Red Army base areas in different, often remote, areas of China. Each base area had a fair degree of autonomy in how they were to balance the different policies, land redistribution versus rent reduction, who they let join the Party, and the relation with the KMT and other local military forces. Thus the Communist Party emerged into power with a more federal structure and more regional power brokers. Sinologists tell us that that has been maintained, and some argue that there's always been a majority or near-majority of regional

Party chiefs at the highest levels of power. If they unite, then it is their policy that is implemented and not that of a central Party apparatus. That element has provided a bridge to a more decentralized economy.

JAH: It's also the case, is it not, that the character of the revolution meant that the revolutionaries were forced to live in the countryside for longer periods of time, thereby becoming more capable of seeing what might or might not work?

MM: That was specifically important in the period in which growth was coming from the Township and Village Enterprises; local enterprises initially dominated. Together with local entrepreneurial families, they developed initially small but very dynamic industries providing a substantial amount of growth. The base from which the economy took off was one provided by a Soviet-style command economy but with decentralized Chinese characteristics. The former ensured that literacy, the basic health of the population, mortality rates, and a certain level of industrial production improved under communism. It is well established across the world that when you are engaged in catch-up, some form of state planning is actually very useful, whether it's capitalist planning, as in Japan or Korea, or a communist command structure. It produced substantial industrial development. But it was the latter characteristics that put China in a much better position to develop decentralized competitive industrial structures that are often assumed to be only characteristic of capitalism.

There is probably another contributing factor that is impossible to measure, and that is the fact that it has long been a highly civilized society. We see in general that economic development today in what we used to call "the South" of the world is very much related to whether there was a great civilization there in the past, as in India and most of East and Southeast Asia. The only one that is not doing as well as it should do is the Islamic world, where the curse of the oil rentier state is a contributing factor to stagnation. Other less successful regions had their generally lesser level of civilization wiped out by the European empires, as in Latin America and Africa. Rebuilding after decolonialism there proved more difficult.

JAH: At the moment there is general admiration—and in certain quarters fear—about China. It is often noted that sometime soon China will take the place of Japan as the second-largest economy in the world. But the counter-argument surely remains: that the standard of living per person in China, measured in GDP terms, is still extraordinarily low. Is such a country really capable of challenging? In economic life it is often still a sophisticated area of assembly rather than a heartland of industrial research. It's still rather weak in many ways, isn't it?

MM: What you say is true about per-capita GDP and per-capita income, which is still low and will take a long time to get up to anywhere near, say, American standards. The level of domestic inequality is also large. When one sees in Beijing and Shanghai Lamborghini dealers just a few streets away from slums, then one goes into the countryside and sees the degree of poverty, one realizes that this is an extraordinarily varied country. It is also a country of high savings, partly because there is not much welfare. Citizens must make provisions for their own old age, and their savings are very useful for economic development. It means that China is not particularly dependent on foreign capital. They have been dependent on foreign enterprise and technology, but there isn't any reason why there can't be technology transfer, as was the case with Japan. The other distinctive feature about China, which has played an increasing role in economic development, is overseas Chinese business, which has long dominated regional trade across East and Southeast Asia. The level of foreign investment by overseas Chinese is slightly ahead of that of either the United States or Europe. Since much of the technological dynamism comes from foreign-owned firms, including the overseas Chinese, more technology transfer will be required. But it seems, for example, that in the development of alternative energy sources the Chinese are not lagging behind the United States.

So I don't see any necessary reason why they can't carry on developing. The leadership seems to have sensed in the last few years that they have neglected the countryside and that inequality and diversity are causing too much disorder. Disorder in the form of strikes, demonstrations, and riots is occurring. It is not something that is easy to correct quickly but the regime is aware that some improvement in social citizenship is necessary. Civil and political rights are another matter.

JAH: Presumably another advantage is that it is much more ethnically homogenous. It does not have the problems that the Soviet Union faced. Still, there is the potential for great social strains, which might yet lead to political problems, given the absence of institutional reform. But I admit that the way in which the Party seems to be able to stay on its feet, both by purging itself and by becoming more technocratic, is extraordinary.

MM: China is 90 percent Han Chinese, which is an advantage for social cohesion. The Chinese Communist Party is also committed fundamentally to order and economic growth, and its perception is that for order the unity of the Party is basic. Whatever disagreements they have, and they have always had many disagreements, they won't let them produce the disabling factionalism that accompanied the fall of the Soviet Union. In fact, their discipline has been strengthened by what happened in the Soviet Union as well as by their own Cultural Revolution period. Factions in the end stick by whatever policy is proclaimed officially by the Party. That was already evident in the Civil War period.

JAH: And they also had the historic experience of warring regions when the Chinese Empire collapsed in 1911.

MM: Sure, and the respect that is still shown for Mao as the uniter of the country is an important part of the sense of danger and how to avert it.

JAH: Well, let's turn to the two other BRIC countries, taken in turn, but bearing in mind a particular theory: namely, the one claiming that forcible development depends upon centralizing power so as to educate and to plan, a functional need likely thereby to place democracy at a discount. Indian democracy does seem to have limited economic growth for much of the postwar period, at least in comparison to the record of authoritarian China. What can we say about the Indian case?

MM: India, too, built up a potentiality for economic development on the basis of an economy that had a considerable dose of planning. Though India is a remarkably flourishing democracy, considering the vastness of the country and the diversity of the population, there was elite unity for a considerable period of time. The Congress Party was attracted not exactly to socialism, but to a local variant of the mixed economy. It was relatively secular, but yet Hindu. That provided core unity among the elites, which enabled them to cope with the enormous diversity of the country.

JAH: Successful nationalist struggle is part of that, and, in institutional terms, the presence of the Indian army and the considerable level of bureaucratic skill passed on by the British. But literacy doesn't reach down nearly as far as in the Chinese case. In that sense, India still has tremendous problems in creating a general population able to swim in the modern world.

MM: Its inequality parallels that of China, though here it is reinforced by more illiteracy and greater autonomy and power for property owners in rural areas. As in other East Asian countries there has been a gradual emergence out of the plan toward a more decentralized, market-driven economy. There is a greater degree of insularity than in China: a lower level of foreign trade, a lower dependence on external financing. External financing may not be much of a boost to growth. A few recent studies have shown an inverse relationship internationally. The more foreign capital you receive, the less you develop, which is a very interesting finding.

JAH: The Russian case is relevant here: large amounts of foreign capital received, still more exported by the elite to Western banks! The final case is Brazil, where the dictum of the military regime in 1964 was indeed "order through progress." Furthermore, it had a developmentalist ideology, Comteanism! You can still see Positivist chapels.

MM: Here I have to admit ignorance. I don't know why Brazil has had a recent phase of high economic growth, and I'm not quite sure as yet why it is put among the BRICs. It is a big country . . .

JAH: . . . and it has enormous natural resources. Indeed, all of the countries we've discussed are in fact huge in territorial terms.

A general comment needs to be made about the BRICs. They may have more unity than you suggested earlier. They seem to act together in such places as the WTO. The United States originally created, and sometimes has been able to change, the rules under which the world political economy works. Do the BRICs have enough power to seriously challenge that?

MM: Well, they have the power to stall agreements, as they have shown in the WTO. Some of them have acted collectively there, though together with other developing countries, as they have in climate change issues. We must remember that many poorer and even middle-income countries have limited diplomatic staffs and expert advisors. They are not capable of fielding delegations to international conferences. I know an Egyptian diplomat who on various UNESCO occasions effectively represents the whole of Africa because no other country has the resources to send a representative. China has played an important role in the climate change conferences. It has a large and expert delegation on whom the poorer countries of the South have relied in order to present their case. There is a well-known conflict of interest in terms of who is polluting the world. Is it the advanced countries, who certainly polluted it more in the past up to now, or is it the developing countries as they industrialize, causing increasing pollution? China still represents poorer countries' interests, though it is getting richer. So ganging-up is beginning on issues like trade and tariffs, global warming, the environment, and soon probably finance, but this is rarely organized by the BRIC countries collectively.

JAH: We've been talking about these countries sociologically, in terms of their own political economies. But one theory about the recent financial crisis is an economic theory, held notably by Ben Bernanke, claiming that global imbalances have done much to determine the fate of individual countries. The huge Chinese savings were lent to the United States through the purchase of Treasury bonds, which then allowed interest rates to be very low, creating the housing boom that was a precondition for the recent crisis. Keynes's original plan for the world economy at the end of the war was to penalize creditor countries as much as debtor countries. Do the rules for the world economy need somehow to be regulated to deal with this problem? The same point can be made about the European Union: namely, that Greece is not entirely to blame—it was partly excess German savings seeking an outlet.

MM: But there aren't the institutions built to think like that and to regulate the world economy as a whole. The Chinese Communist Party leadership has decided that it is in its interest to put more into domestic expansion, but I don't expect the problems of global imbalances to suddenly be removed like this.

JAH: Well, it's very complicated. The United States sometimes pushes China to save less and consume more, so that it can revive its own export industries, but it needs Chinese capital to effectively deal with the next years. So it's a very tricky matter, and there are, I agree, no institutions, for the world economy and within the EU, capable of dealing with this.

I have a couple of questions concerning particular countries as agents of change, but with concentration now on regions and types. The EU claims a measure of unity as a group. Is there any chance that this unit could challenge the United States? The United States was for a long period protective, and that really mattered enormously for initial European integration. But the end of the Cold War allowed parts of the European establishment to imagine a world in which the United States played a lesser role. American support still matters to the Baltic states and to Poland; they have not forgotten their membership in the Soviet empire, and they still feel there is a sense of threat. Donald Rumsfeld used this difference when the second Iraq war was being discussed, so as to distinguish "old" from "new" Europe. This suggests a lack of unity within Europe. And I happen to think that Europeans in general still want the American presence, even though they sometimes complain about its costs. So I don't see a challenge here.

MM: Can the EU act as a unit? Sometimes, though not often. However, in questions of climate change it has produced a common framework of policy, even if it allows for voluntary targets and compliance from its member states. Here it has also developed leadership claims, and its policies are indeed a little more advanced than others. However, in Copenhagen in December 2009 the US and China slapped down the EU leadership claims. It was their minimal deal, and not the more developed proposals of the Europeans, that was half-endorsed by the Climate Change Conference.

The EU also has internal problems. There are clearly many people within the European institutions, and among the political class in Europe more generally, who would like federalism to develop further, but there has been a popular reaction against that in recent years. The history of referenda over the last twenty years has not been a good one for the federal project. There have been more referenda defeats than victories, so that reforms are now being legislated within parliaments without directly consulting the electorate and governments have become more cautious. So I think that the European Union for the near future is stalled at the level it has reached at present. It has new permanent officials, the head and the foreign secretary. But they are relative unknowns, and they cannot mobilize the European Union as a whole. The EU doesn't really exist as a coherent actor in relation to the rest of the world, except in defense of interests that became entrenched some time ago, as in agriculture, hijacked by the agricultural interests of a few countries. Agriculture still counts for a very substantial part of the European budget.

JAH: Yes, and one must add that the Union's budget is any case tiny—something like 1 percent of Europe's GDP.

MM: There are no collective armed forces. In 2009, when France was making economic cuts in its defense budget, it made cuts, seemingly unwittingly, that had the effect of bringing back to France the French forces of the Franco-German brigade that were stationed in Germany. When that was publicized, the French government had to hastily say that this wasn't happening, but it showed the kind of priorities involved. The geopolitical and military weakness of the EU is very well known, while its weakness as a geo-economic actor is being exposed in the second phase of the current great recession.

JAH: It is very odd for leading countries to have a single currency without a political union, something that has never been tried before. And there is potential for great conflict, since some large countries, notably Britain, do not belong to that shared currency. Having said all that, though, there is an achievement about which Europeans can be extraordinarily proud. If one thinks of foreign policy successes in the last forty years, nothing can rival the entry into the EU of new states from Southern Europe first, and then from Central Europe.

MM: And the encouragement of democracy. US governments talk all the time about the expansion of
democracy. Europeans have been much, much more
successful in their eastward extension of democracy.
Some European social scientists use the word "empire"
when discussing the expansion of the EU, but I don't
think that is appropriate. Expansion has been dominated by incentives offered and desire to join, not
coercion. True, there are conditions. The economic
incentives are assumed to be large, in return for which
new countries will do certain things, including democratization. We see the impact of it right across Eastern
Europe and Turkey, and it's the most significant extension of democracy in recent years.

JAH: Yes, and potentially the most stable extension—
although it will take time for some of the less prepared
countries, Bulgaria and Romania above all, to consoli-
date fully.

MM: Of course, these countries had already experienced
some rather imperfect democracy in the interwar
period, and it is easier for some to be democratic now
because minority ethnic issues are of much lower
salience today. Unfortunately, massive ethnic cleansing
of minorities took place in the war and in its
aftermath.

JAH: Let us turn away from potential challengers, to the
excluded. What about Latin America?

MM: One interesting development in Latin America is the
much-delayed emergence of claims on citizenship by
the indigenous people, above all in the Andean countries. That has shifted politics more to the left, toward
a rough coalition between the representatives of indigenous peoples and the old left. This is having an impact

and it's also reducing the power of the US in South America.

JAH: So Bolivia and Ecuador are engaged in basic nation building, putting them at a different stage of history than India or China?

MM: The pattern of conquest, superimposing class differences on ethnic differences, including imported slaves, produced very high inequality of landholding. The relative absence of international war meant taxes were low, popular movements focused less on the state, and states remained weak and factionalized. All of that has held back the continent in the middle of the twentieth century. But now, as you say, there is a consolidation of nation-states as indigenous peoples are demanding full citizenship. The proximity and overwhelming power of the US in the hemisphere has always been a problem, but the problem has shifted from the Marines to drugs. Both Columbia and Mexico are being deeply corroded by the problem of their proximity to the American consumption of drugs.

JAH: That transnational flow presents a problem for social scientists, still largely reliant on national statistics, not least as the sums involved are supposed to be huge.

MM: It's presumably the biggest global industry, and may well be followed by the arms market, and these don't appear in international statistics since illegal flows are the most genuinely transnational part of contemporary capitalism. Peasants find it much more profitable to grow opium or cannabis and sell it to smugglers. Since it is an illicit trade it involves its own paramilitary forces. In Colombia it was initially connected to a land war, with left-wing guerrillas defending peasants' rights. In Mexico it doesn't have that connection, but it's currently destroying a fair amount of the

Mexican state, the political parties, and the police system.

JAH: There is, of course, a great variety inside Latin America, Chile having a particular pattern that looks relatively successful now, Argentina cursed by a populist pattern that has led—uniquely—to its losing the position it once held as one of the most advanced countries in the world.

Thinking about variety allows us to turn to failed states. This concept seems to me to be loose and amorphous. Most of the cases that people have in mind are small countries that never had much infrastructural power, but the term just as clearly applies to the Soviet Union! Then there is the fact that some states fail and then recover. So let us try to be more specific, beginning with Arab states—not, let me make clear, Muslim states, some of which have rather successful growth rates. Is that likely to change? It might be useful to remember the old view, now discredited, that insisted that Catholicism held back development in Latin America. It is sometimes claimed that the position of women—especially low levels of literacy with great consequences for fertility patterns—is a huge developmental block. What do you think?

MM: You raise a number of issues there. In the Middle East one must distinguish the oil-producing states from the others. The former have the particular problem of a state that actually owns this predominant source of wealth and where there is, therefore, no significant civil society separated from the state. The state has the only major source of wealth so it does not need to tax, and its subjects therefore do not develop strong claims for citizenship in return. They are supplicants at the court of the state and the state distributes patronage to those whose loyalty it needs. As far as the non-oil-producing countries are concerned, most also tend to have narrowly based patronage states. Only in Iran and Turkey have broad-based middle class groups (*bazaari*, merchant-artisan groups) and some workers been able to press for more representative government. There is also a problem of secular illiteracy in Arab-speaking countries where the Koran dominates and production of other books is very low. There have been obvious failures of oppositional movements. Arab socialism, Arab nationalism, and military regimes didn't produce anything better.

JAH: Part of the explanation presumably is that they are semi-militarized, feeling that they have to react to Israel because of the Palestinian question, a factor that distorts the pattern of social development in the region. There is an unsolved geopolitical problem here, making it wholly different from the other areas of the world that we have discussed.

MM: This is true of non-oil producers, the Lebanon, Syria, Jordan, and Egypt, which are Israel's neighbors and which have been involved in generally losing wars against Israel, and which maintain large militaries. Of course, Egypt and Jordan now get substantial American aid so that they will not fight Israel, but so far that foreign aid isn't producing very much in the way of development, and it seems that the Egyptian regime is becoming more rather than less authoritarian.

JAH: In the African case there is also great variety, although there is a general sense of a social world held together by external agreement to maintain state boundaries, thereby protecting very weak states bereft of much national consolidation.

MM: Here the legacy of colonialism remains fairly strong. There are one or two areas where white settlers became very numerous, but for the most part the countries were developed only to the extent that there were important natural resources. Some regions had intensive cash-crop agriculture, plantations and minerals, and were connected to the capital, which was normally a port, by a rail line or by a river. But most of the hinterland, the bulk of the territory, was not in any real sense controlled by the colonial power and was left substantially on its own.

Now the colonial powers have departed and the surplus of the profitable areas is no longer shipped mainly to London or to Paris, but it is still shipped out by the only infrastructures to the international economy as a whole. Once again the hinterland is not much connected. Only in the very last stages of the British and French empires during World War II and just after was there much investment in development, and this created a more educated urban middle class and an industrial labor force. This didn't help the colonial powers, since these sectors developed labor unions and urban opposition movements which formed the basis of African nationalism. The colonial powers were thrown out by their own creations. But the new nationalism was and still is paper-thin. Moreover, now if a region has valuable resources, its local elites can decide that they have alternative means of getting the resources to global markets without going through the state and its capital. That generates civil war situations and further state weakening. The notion of a "failed state" is used too broadly across Africa, but the norm is a weak state where the urban population is bought off by the regime since it can cause coups, while rural elites make their own particularistic deals with the capital. Perhaps India and China will help domestic development more than the Europeans did.

JAH: So your judgment here is that the distortions of these countries, their lack of development, is partly the result of the way in which their empires treated them?

MM: I think so, though to sustain the argument would require some serious counterfactual history of what would have happened without colonialism. It did hurt these countries because it destroyed existing political structures, and though these were not usually very strong, they were at least indigenous, producing some regulation of local social relations. So had Africa been left alone, I guess that some of that regulation, some political structures, would have gradually developed further, boosting more production and trade, at first on a regional basis, then more broadly. Colonial development, by destroying existing institutions and not replacing them with anything comparable, probably did harm the continent. And that seems to be the conclusion of most of those who have attempted quantitative analysis, correlating years of colonialism to economic development—though of course the statistics are lousy.

JAH: I now have a very disturbing question, following on from an earlier exchange. The final move toward economic and political development in the advanced world seems to have rested on the creation of relatively homogenous ethnic nations. One would hate to see African countries following the European pattern of homogenization through ethnic cleansing in the midst of war. Can you imagine that these countries might develop institutions to allow them to successfully develop polities with a multinational character?

MM: Well, first we have to take encouragement from the last couple of decades. Though we do still use the terms North and South of the world, a fair number of countries are successfully developing and it's a far cry from the period when development seemed generally blocked and plausible theories of "dependent development" and "unequal exchange" assumed that a condition of the success of the North was the failure of the South. So the rise of East Asia, Southeast Asia, South Asia, Eastern Europe, Brazil, South Africa and a few other African countries has to be regarded as encouraging.

Second, though homogeneity seems to help a little, it is not strictly necessary. India is the great exception, but Brazil is another one. Third, European movement away from multi-ethnic to mono-ethnic states was very much connected with their imperial rivalries, and with their defeat or exhaustion in war. Multi-ethnic states seemed not to be as good at war as more mono-ethnic ones—at least that is generally what political leaders themselves concluded. But international war is now relatively infrequent. It's infrequent in Africa. European history is the greatest example of international war, not Latin America or Africa.

The vast bulk of African wars are civil wars. About half of them have somewhat of an ethnic character—though I suspect that underlying most of the civil wars, ethnic or not, are interregional disputes about power resources. Since we only get bad news in our media about Africa, we often do not realize that most African states are not riven by famines or civil wars. Indeed, multi-ethnicity is not generally very dangerous. If there are many ethnic groups, then government has to involve coalitions between at least several among them. The dangerous cases—as I argued in *The Dark Side of Democracy*—are bi-ethnic or tri-ethnic countries, in which one group can form a government and discriminate against the other. Even so, really dire consequences only emerge where the discriminated group feels it can resist, which is normally the case only where it can get help from abroad. This was the case in Rwanda. In the Sudan pressure is exerted from environmental change, as desertification pushed Arab pastoralists southward onto African agriculturalists in

Darfur. These are not typical of Africa, or of any other continent.

JAH: Has war in the modern world changed its character so that it is these rather weak states with ethnic divisions in them that will be the sites of conflict?

MM: But at any one point in time only a few African states are experiencing civil war, only in a handful does it seem endemic—the Sudan, Somalia, the Congo—and even they may be solvable. African states have a common interest in preventing secessions, since they might all become vulnerable if it became easy. Diplomatic institutions have already helped reduce the instances of international war. The major problem is that when development happens, if it takes a regional basis, which it often does with natural resources—oil, for example—then strife easily develops between regions, as is the case in Nigeria. Regional inequality may produce the possibility of a province claiming autonomy or independence.

7

Group Agency

JAH: Let us look at agency in the modern world in a different way, by turning from states to the actions of particular social groups. As background, one should remember your longstanding sociological insight: that the forcefulness of social movements depends upon possessing some grand conception of the world, some sense of totality. You have consistently argued that this does not come from purely economic difference, but rather as the result of political exclusion by a state, which unifies sentiment and so creates force within a group. In a nutshell, social movements take on the color of the states with which they interact. For instance, differential levels of class cohesion resulted from state behavior, with total exclusion in Russia creating, at times, workers who were genuinely socially revolutionary.

In contrast, your recent work on the Great Depression in the United States makes much of powerful popular forces capable of producing "lib–lab" social change even though the state was not exclusionary. Isn't this a contradiction?

MM: No, I don't think there is a contradiction because Russian workers were wholly excluded and generated revolutionary movements, while American workers were only partially excluded and so developed reformist movements operating with and around existing power structures. In the US quite moderate labor unions already existed and they now expanded, alongside more lib–lab reformism in what was already a white male democracy (including workers) built around two major political parties. Workers were not politically excluded, but their capacity to form unions and influence congressmen and senators in urban-industrial states helped effect a partial transformation of the parties into being class parties. The Democratic Party became the party of labor, with the decline of Progressive Republicans, and the Republican Party confirmed itself as the party of business. The South does not fit this model since race remained there the primary political axis.

JAH: So straightforward class weight—above all, high levels of unionization—plus the experience of the Great Depression were capable of producing significant pressure from below, leading to serious reform?

MM: Reform, yes. They were also assisted because unemployment rose to almost a third of the labor force and that affected the living standards of an awful lot of people. For example, in industrial areas landlords, shopkeepers, and the like suffered because people weren't buying their goods or paying their rent. There was a broader wave of sympathy so that it was not merely class-based. The growth of the labor unions, the growth of the militancy in the industrial working class was probably the vanguard but there was a lot of popular support for reform by ordinary people. So populists and pragmatic liberal politicians like President Roosevelt or Senator Wagner saw their opportunity to win elections on a reform agenda.

JAH: So sometimes working-class movements may become popular movements capable of pushing through reform?

MM: Certainly in the period of the middle of the twentieth century, and the immediate postwar period, where we are still talking about industrial societies. There was a subtle transformation of the working class into the popular classes and then into the people.

JAH: That was a preface to asking you about present circumstances, in which union rates in very large numbers of advanced capitalist countries have fallen dramatically, especially outside public employment. There is a good deal of variation of course. Still, has the working-class-to-popular movement lost its capacity for good?

MM: Well, it depends which countries of the world you are talking about. If you're talking about the advanced countries in Europe, then the forward movement of the working class amid a broader left-leaning populism has clearly ended for the foreseeable future. There's defense of existing institutions, but not much more than that.

JAH: Defense can be quite powerful, not least as it can include new elements: women in Scandinavia, for example, keen to protect their social rights together with a more general concern about health coverage. But it is defensive, seeking to conserve what has been gained.

MM: There are now far more women in labor movements than in the past because there are far more women in the full-time labor market and because women have also pressed for broader citizenship through the twentieth century. But feminism and the American Civil Rights Movement have tended to shift oppositional politics somewhat away from class issues toward what is called identity politics. These have broadened to other forms of personal identity, such as sexual preference and disability.

Identity politics tend to focus on equal civil and political rights more than on social equality, at least to begin with. The Anglophone countries have seen the biggest retreat in the labor movement. We see in the United States the growth of a rival rightist populism, somewhat anti-big business but more strongly anti-big government. Some of the causes of labor's decline are underlying forces, like the shift from industry to services, which means that workers tend to be in smaller work units, with increasing numbers in more casual forms of employment, and these situations are not conducive to unionization. There has not really occurred a strengthening of middle-class leftism. So the prospects do not look good for the labor movements. It does seem that this was a twentieth-century phenomenon, which will not be such a major player in the advanced countries in the next century.

JAH: Politics go in cycles and one shouldn't over-generalize. Still, in the midst of a very serious recession the left is not doing very well, both in terms of countries turning to the right, but also in terms of the absence of a leftist reaction.

MM: The experience of the Great Depression was that every single government that was in power at the beginning of the Depression lost power, except for the Canadian government. In some countries that meant a move to the left, as in the United States or Sweden, but some countries saw a move to the right, as in Britain and Australia, and it involved a swing to fascism in Germany and to militarism in Japan. But all were capable of considerable popular mobilization—there was populism of both the left and the right. This current great recession has not lasted as long. It may eventually have similar effects, but one difference is the lack of opposition within the finance sector itself. It's not a unionized sector, nor a very working-class one. Finance also seems abstruse and distant to most people. It's not like the Great Depression in that respect. Unemployment comes, but it comes indirectly; you don't know quite whom to blame. It's not very long since there were enormous protest movements across the South of the world against structural adjustment programs, and there's nothing comparable now. So this is not a recession that seems to raise much direct class conflict. There is resentment against bankers, but it does not connect to a leftist or a rightist populist movement. The arguments are technical, left to elites.

JAH: Bankers aren't states: they are not, in a way, directly doing things to you. They're harder to locate.

MM: Right. Now, doubtless, if this continues, governments across the world will be kicked out because they will be blamed, but it still feels very different.

JAH: I have a general comment about your recent work. I detect your becoming irritated at the way in which modern sociology ignores class factors, both when dealing with liberal reforms and when describing the character of nationalism. Am I right to characterize you in this way?

MM: Class always matters. We're talking now about the decline of the working class, but the capitalist class is alive and kicking us. Marxists have the great virtue of reminding us of that, even if they are somewhat one-dimensional in their analysis. The neglect by sociology of the power of capital in our society is indefensible.

Of course, some are discussing it but most sociologists are not, and some even believe that "class is dead." On the other hand, there is a tendency among people who do pay attention to class to exaggerate the capitalist class's degree of transnational capacity, to talk about a global capitalist class. I think on the contrary that it remains a dual entity: though there are strong transnational elements they entwine with strong national structuring of capitalism, which, after all, needs and benefits from state regulation.

JAH: Two other classes deserve consideration. The first is that of the traditional landed upper class—"old regime" members, in your appellation. There seems to be something of a divide here. Sometimes old regimes could act as a force for democratization—by organizing popular conservative parties, as in Great Britain. But they were more often weak and scared, sometimes staying in power through divide-and-rule tactics, at other times trying to mobilize people below in their own projects, often nationalist in character. You have theoretical observations about this from time to time. Is it possible to have a general theory about upper classes in this way?

MM: The old regime was very important during the first half of the twentieth century. Non-fascist authoritarian regimes were dominated by them. They came to a deal with Mussolini; they couldn't control Hitler, but they were important in his rise. In countries with old institutions, like Great Britain, they survived in democratic form into the postwar period, but I think that they've been largely finished off by the Thatcher revolution. Dominant elites in Britain now are essentially capitalist ones. I think that, in a curious kind of way, in the American South a kind of old regime remains.

JAH: Overrepresented in the military?

MM: Yes, but also in controlling the Southern political process. No longer planters, but merchants and local professional elites, not just capitalists.

JAH: The ability of old regimes to adapt to capitalism, rather than to oppose it, has happened in Europe, I agree, but it's a current problem in large parts of the world.

MM: And in Latin America old regime groups remain strong. There have never been land reforms in most of the hemisphere, and significant differences in wealth are still related to possession of land and its resources— and the state. There old regimes survive quite well, partly because they were propped up by the United States against the supposed threat of communism. It is different in some of East Asia, where landed classes and old regimes have been compromised by their association with the European and Japanese empires. After the war there was land reform and the power of old-regime elites in various countries was weakened.

JAH: So let's turn to a final class question, this time concerning peasants. You see late-twentieth-century revolutions as dependent upon peasants. This had not been true necessarily of other revolutions, which I will ask you about in a moment. Is it likely that peasants will have the capacity to act as a class in the future, or are they doomed to extinction by development? Was it a particular moment when peasants were able to act as a class?

MM: There was a wave of peasant revolutions from mid-twentieth-century China onward. The Chinese showed that revolution was possible, that the old regime had lost the mandate of heaven. It had needed the contingencies of war to be successful, but the fusion of rural class struggle and national struggle against foreign imperialism carried Chinese influence across Southeast Asia. Left to domestic forces, all of Korea would have fallen, and all of Vietnam did. The Latin American cases are somewhat separate from that. They originated as attempts to get land reforms in rural areas, and since you couldn't do that without attacking the state, they attacked the state, too, though they were rarely successful.

JAH: There was a moment when leftist thinkers felt you could adopt Maoism and have peasant revolutions in large parts of the world. By and large that was a failure.

MM: There were two successful cases in Latin America, Cuba and Nicaragua—which was then undermined by an extraordinary degree of American intervention. Indeed, the declining power of revolutions owes something to the counter-revolutionary role of the United States. Not only revolutionaries learned lessons. After Korea the US determined to confront revolutionaries with all necessary force, even to "scorched earth tactics" which would kill many thousands and destroy the credibility of communist regimes. After Korea or Vietnam or Nicaragua, which neighbors would want to emulate their leftists and try to seize power? The current thinking on theories of revolution is to downplay insurgent strength and emphasize the weakness of the old regime state, with personalist dictatorships being potentially the most vulnerable. It is almost impossible for a movement in the countryside to overthrow an urban-based government, unless there are very significant splits within that government. This may be true, but United States foreign policy made peasant revolution, or any other leftist revolution, less likely.

JAH: Just two more questions about "group agency." One question concerns intellectuals, mostly as revolutionaries. They clearly mattered enormously in the Chinese case in that they had a long period of training, as noted, and were able to make local contacts and change themselves in the process of making a revolution. There are not many cases of intellectuals developing and becoming a force in their own right in quite the same way. Do you agree?

MM: Yes, this was a particular historical wave of Marxism. People with a very strong vision of the future . . .

JAH: And a model to copy, after the success of the Soviet Union.

MM: Yes, after the Soviet Union and its Comintern, which assisted them. Bearing in mind that the working-class part of the original Chinese Communist Party was eliminated by Chiang Kai-shek in the Shanghai massacre of 1927, most of the remaining party elite and the new waves of young recruits who were sent out to the rural areas were students, teachers, and the like. So, yes, this was a movement led at all levels by intellectuals. Of course, they wouldn't have been successful without other conditions, but they had a vision of the future, an ideology, which drove them onward, and a plausible view of major reforms that peasants could appreciate—more land, lower rents and taxes. They initially made the mistake of being too radical; at least that was the conclusion that Mao and others drew from the failure of the first Kiangsi Soviet. So they learned moderate policies of reduction of rent and taxes without confiscation of land, and the value of pragmatic, temporary alliances with some landowners and rival militias. They learned to combine them in different ways, according to the local situation on the ground. So they had an ideology to which they were committed in the end, and that greatly sustained them emotionally and morally, but they also knew that they had to be pragmatic about the means.

JAH: Others who followed the Soviet model were not as pragmatic, and consequently failed?

MM: There was in effect a competition between different models applied in different base areas, and those who failed died. The combination of Marx and Mao then spread for a period through the world, had a few successes but more failures, and then of course it collapsed, as in the Soviet Union, or reformed itself, as in China. So it's probably finished.

JAH: So there was just this one particular historical moment?

MM: Though the right metaphor is a wave, surging across the world, and ending up decades later in the world's far hinterlands, such as Nepal or Chiapas.

JAH: So here was a group of intellectuals made powerful because they had a vision of the world. Presumably one could say the same about some Islamic intellectuals now, or intellectuals in the most general sense, the highly educated in Egypt, or Saudi Arabia, who are historical actors in a significant way.

MM: A weaker parallel case was fascism, but that failed more quickly because of its overreliance on militarism. There was also a broader attempt by African socialism, Arab socialism, by highly educated elites, often army officers, but they didn't yield very good results, and have decayed. And now we have the Muslim alternative to that, the Islamists.

JAH: It's much less capable of organizing a society, it would seem to me.

MM: Because it is not a complete vision; it's incoherent when it comes to economic development questions.

JAH: There's another sense in which one can think of intellectuals, though: as the educated. Development is something of a social evolutionary force, driving forward education and creating universities. It's noticeable that certain revolutionary moments have been deeply influenced by students who are unemployed, as in Iran. There may be more of that in the future. It's very hard to get your manpower planning right, and so you overeducate large amounts of people. Another case would be the "overproduction" of educated Sinhalese, whose lack of employment caused resentment. Isn't this a potential force of instability in the modern world?

MM: Yes, though think of the case of India, where there is an overproduction of graduates, but it doesn't seem to result in disturbances. Although it's possible that Hindu extremists may recruit such people.

JAH: There is one final group to consider: paramilitaries. These actors play a very large role in your account of the twentieth century. The absence of interstate war means that they are not so important in contemporary world politics.

MM: It depends on what part of the world we are discussing. There was a distinct historical origin of European paramilitaries at the beginning of the twentieth century. Even before the war very large numbers of men had been trained in reserve forces and there were also significant drilling organizations in civil society, like the Boy Scouts movement. Then in 1914 came mass-mobilization warfare. After the war, revolutionary turbulence broke out in the defeated countries and many discontented veterans formed paramilitaries, especially on the right, to force through their solutions to the strife. All fascist parties developed from these paramilitaries. Japanese militarism also depended for its

shock troops at home on armed bands of junior officers assassinating moderate generals and politicians.

At the same time in the United States, however, paramilitaries, earlier active against Native Americans and
workers, were largely disappearing (except for the Ku
Klux Klan). There was no flowering of paramilitaries
after World War II since it had resulted in the defeated
powers also being occupied and controlled by the
victors. There was no space for or tolerance of paramilitaries. There was a delayed exception in Yugosla-
via, where the break-up of communism entwined with
ethnic conflict in which paramilitaries composed of
men accustomed to bearing arms came to figure large.
Nowadays there is insignificant paramilitarism in the
advanced countries.

It is different elsewhere. The paramilitaries that have
formed have usually been in response to civil war,
often taking an ethnic form. Some of them in Africa
and Asia contain child soldiers. In Africa paramilitaries have become especially active, helped by the international trade in small arms. Some state armed forces
are effectively irregulars, too. The extent of paramilitarism is one reason I separate military from political
power, of course.

8

Outcomes

JAH: I'm going to turn toward outcomes of recent history to see if one can discover trends that suggest repetitions in the future. Let's start by remembering that war is seen in your account of the recent past as a powerful force for social change. Let me give an example. Your explanation of the divergence between Britain and the United States after World War II rests on a contrast between the solidarity created in Britain by participation in a "people's war" and its absence in the United States—which was not attacked on its own soil, and therefore lacked the solidarity on the base of which further reform could be pushed forward. Do I have that right?

MM: With one qualification: American military veterans got the G.I. Bill of Rights, since those who really did sacrifice in World War II got significant welfare benefits. That was a more traditional form of welfare, more like Wilhelmine Germany, where ex-soldiers were given government jobs.

JAH: And in Europe there is a strong relationship between war and social reform, affecting even those countries which did not engage in war. This leads in Europe to an historic class compromise after 1945, resulting in a general regime of welfare and liberal citizenship.

MM: Neutral countries which stayed neutral were nonetheless seriously affected. Rationing was introduced amid a sense of common suffering, which was also a boost to welfare. Whatever encouraged the solidarity of the nation helped welfare states. The grand compromise in continental Europe was different. What had happened as a result of the war was that the far right had been eliminated, or disabled because people resented what devastation they had wrought. Nazis obviously continued to survive in senior positions, but they couldn't really do very much other than pursue their own personal interests. As a project, fascism was over.

In most countries the extreme left had been destroyed as well. This was most obviously the case in West Germany. France and Italy were different, since communists had figured large in wartime resistance movements, and in Greece there was a civil war. But by and large, there was a common project of economic reconstruction and a great incentive for a compromise between the respectable right, often Christian Democrats, and the moderate left, the Socialist Party. The Catholic Church finally made peace with the center left. Its "social Christianity" infused Christian Democrat parties with aspirations that were compatible with social democracy. What these countries failed to achieve in the first half of the century suddenly became possible for them, with the removal of the far right and the far left. In the case of France and Italy it also involved some discrediting of communism, with the help of the United States. In the case of Greece it involved repression by military force, with the help of the British.

But in general, there was a grand compromise and it was successful and it endured. And whereas World

War II had intensified progressive taxation in the liberal countries, in most of Europe it brought progressive welfare states. These remained alternative ways of achieving greater social citizenship.

JAH: There is a sense in which it is depressing to see that this formation owes so much to the character of the wars in Europe in the twentieth century. Modernization theorists suggesting that the European model will be copied everywhere are probably wrong. One can imagine a logic perhaps leading to education, but the complete European model, varied as it is, needed war to get it going. Doesn't that suggest it cannot be replicated elsewhere?

MM: Maybe, though I think we have to be a little cautious because there are other possible routes available. The two world wars certainly produced immense dislocation and shifts of direction, though as far as the advanced countries are concerned, the long-term trajectory of development of social citizenship is also discernible, provided the left was able to harness its progressive policies to a sense of national solidarity. That was the Nordic route, and it was the one least affected by war. Provided the surge of working-class leftism could find broader national resonance—and the other major crisis, the Great Depression, assisted this in some countries—social citizenship was on the way up. Unless there was serious exclusion of the working class, some form of class compromise was likely. The forms of compromise that emerged were just visible already before World War I. The liberal version, government staying out of labor relations, was already established in Britain (though not the US, where government was still selectively repressing labor). The Nordic countries already had the elements of what one might call corporatism, greater involvement of the state in collective bargaining. Catholicism had already developed a small social Christian wing. Churches,

Bismarckians, and Liberals (like David Lloyd George) were already trying to head off socialism by flourishing social programs. The first stirrings of welfare programs had emerged in virtually all countries. The elements were there, but their combination and international and macro-regional variations were not. They were enabled to develop with the aid of the three great crises of the first half of the twentieth century.

The more general question is what would the world have been like without the two great wars? This involves a large set of counter-factuals. It is easiest to perceive alternative outcomes in China and in geopolitics. In China without war there would probably have been a Nationalist victory in the Civil War, and a continuing Japan–China standoff in Asia, with the balance of power eventually shifting away from Japan (which has happened anyway). Elsewhere, the power of Germany would probably have remained great, not rivaling the economic power of the US, but geopolitically perhaps its equal; Britain, France, and others would have lost their empires and power more gradually, which might have been better for the development of their ex-colonies. Can we envisage a milder form of fascism enduring, no European Union, the American New Deal persisting longer (since the war, on balance, set it back)? Maybe. They are real possibilities.

But what we do know is that they are unlikely to be repeated. Either another major war would cause near-total destruction or no more major wars would occur, therefore no sudden and major challenges would be thrust at the world from military power relations. And in that sense it may be harder for major structural changes to occur, or at least it would be harder to dislodge existing power elites. There probably won't be much change as a result of this great recession. The Chinese Communist Party may well be able to hold onto power for a long period of time. The somewhat corrupted forms of democracy, including that in the United States, may have greater durability than we expect. Globalization will continue within capitalist and nation-state bounds, though gradually becoming freed from American dominance.

JAH: Very often intellectuals like the drama of radical change, there being romanticism about ideas involving the creation of new worlds. Of course, intellectuals ought to remember that ideational change involved not just Bolshevism but also fascism. So maybe a less dramatic world, duller and more conservative in some ways, would at least avoid disaster. You can't calculate these moral equations, but change is not always necessarily good.

MM: No, of course not. But we're talking about the grand compromise, stabilizing social relations to end catastrophes like world wars, fascism, and the Holocaust.

JAH: It may well be that war sped up what might have happened anyway. But in another area—revolutions—it seems to me that the role of war is primary. Would the revolutions of the twentieth century been possible without the impact of war in defeating regimes?

MM: That's certainly true of the major communist revolutions. War was a necessary condition of the Russian revolutions, of the Chinese revolution, the Vietnamese. It's not true of Cuba or Iran or one or two minor cases. But orthodox comparative sociology, counting every revolution as an equal case, is rather misleading. Two successful revolutions, the Bolshevik and the Chinese, changed the world and they were induced by war. Further industrial development in Czarist Russia, if there wasn't a change of the attitude of the regime, would have produced a revolution, but it would have been suppressed. The Chinese Communist Party would not have survived if Japan hadn't attacked China. It distracted Chiang Kai-shek, who was just in the process of eliminating the Communists.

JAH: Great sociologists, Tocqueville for example, have claimed that revolutions would become rarer in modern circumstances. In a way you're saying the same thing, albeit by stressing the importance of geo-politics rather than the impact of consumer culture. Do you agree that as long as there are no major wars, revolutions are less likely, or perhaps *always* unlikely?

MM: Or some major dislocation equivalent to war.

JAH: What would that be?

MM: An environmental crisis that was not solved by collective international negotiation, which might lead to actual wars, or alternatively to massive regime disloca-tions and diminishing state power to repress, resulting in revolutions of the right or left.

JAH: But barring that, the prospect for revolutionaries is perhaps slim. Che Guevara's insistence that revolutions were always likely in modern circumstances is then completely wrong? After all, he was himself killed.

MM: He wasn't going to win in Bolivia.

JAH: Anywhere?

MM: Probably not, but partly because the US played a role in suppressing revolutions in the postwar period. It was willing to destroy in order to deter. So even if you didn't defeat the communist in Vietnam, you've made

Vietnam so unlivable that neighbors were not going to be making the same move. Similarly, you fight a war of attrition and you grind down the regime, as in Nicaragua. The US has also helped suppress revolution to a lesser extent in Colombia.

JAH: The obvious exception to all that you have said is the Shah of Iran, who had an enormous military machine, highly trained and in possession of modern weapons. He still failed. This is something outside the bounds of normal sociological understanding of revolutions.

MM: It's not quite so outside the contemporary theories of revolution, because the Iranian Revolution has been factored into what are now the conventional approaches. The conditions that are generally considered to be necessary are an insurgent movement with a degree of ideological penetration of the urban world; and a factionalized, weakening regime, which is often true in the case of a personalized exclusionary regime. That means an authoritarian ruler, his clique or court, which tends to exclude other power groupings. These are the conditions most likely to lead to revolution. Iran fits this quite well: some economic development, but a large portion of it going to the armed forces and the Shah's own faction. The regime increasingly alienated other elites, including, of course, Islamic elites and much of the middle class. Islamic resistance was especially important because mosques could act as the organizing network of oppositional forces.

JAH: I can see all that, but there's a difference there between a Somoza and the Shah. Somoza's rule was entirely personal—it has usefully been called, using a Weberian term, "Sultanist": his family held key positions, and the army was not run on meritocratic lines. The situation in Iran seems entirely different. The army was genuinely meritocratic, and it had been trained at high levels by the United States with repression in mind. Why was it not prepared to repress?

MM: Well, there is some disagreement among those analyzing the Iranian Revolution. Some say that the popular protest demonstrations had become so enormous that the army felt it couldn't cope. There were some desertions, and some soldiers turned their arms on their own officers. The army felt it could not repress. The other interpretation is that the Shah lost confidence. He was seriously ill and didn't want to leave his young son with a chaotic situation requiring much repression. So he was only able to repress in a half-hearted, inconsistent way, which only encouraged the opposition. In this alternative view the generals are waiting for the order to repress but it doesn't come. Then the Shah leaves the country, and the actual overthrow comes when he's out of the country. This was a personalist regime, and there the person matters.

JAH: As far as the second interpretation is concerned, it is very noticeable that if you do react very brutally—the Chinese in Tiananmen Square, perhaps the situation in Iran now—you can survive. Action matters. But perhaps the other moral, if the first theory you identified is true, is that elites need to divide, the better to rule. You can't alienate everybody at the same time.

MM: True. I think that I would add to that conventional wisdom only that military force is in the last instance the preeminent explanation, and so a divided military or one that is penetrated by popular forces is finally necessary for revolution. Failed, repressed revolutions are much more common than successful ones.

JAH: If you look back at all the horrors of the twentieth century, might it be the case that they did not really change the path of history? The Soviet Union has come and gone, Germany is once again the dominant power on the continent.

MM: If we take the case of the Bolshevik Revolution, it did lead to a fundamentally different history for Russia and the Russian Empire, for the countries around it, and for the world as a whole. And it lasted for 75 years.

JAH: And tens of millions of people were killed in the process. Has it changed the history of the world?

MM: Without a doubt. Without it no Cold War, no revolutions elsewhere, in China, probably a more successful nationalist regime incorporating a strong left element, and therefore, perhaps, a deterrent to Japan. Japan developing as a more normal kind of country. Economic resource bases and infrastructures tend to have an enduring economic capacity: they are long-lived and they can be recovered after wars. So the US was in any case going to be the leading economic power by virtue of its abundant natural resources and its continuous ability to attract skilled human capital. Of course, Germany, if united, would also be a force of global economic power. And certainly Chinese development would have been very different.

JAH: There is one counter-example to the view that social change is heavily indebted to war, namely the rise of neoliberalism. This has changed the heart of capitalist society since the late 1970s. Where did that protean force come from?

MM: I am not saying that *only* war causes social change. But neoliberalism is I think less than protean. It came partly from within the logic of capitalism, partly from its successive domination by Anglophone powers, and partly from the more conservative turn that advanced countries took from the 1970s onward. The economic logic part might fit Polanyi's notion of cycles between relatively market-dominated and relatively statist-dominated phases of capitalism. The other two characteristics do not fit, revealing that cycles are partly illusory, since other developments are simultaneously occurring. The Anglophone cause was the consequence of dominance by liberal powers which had never accepted as much statism as the prior Keynesian phase might have led us to believe. And the conservative turn helps us understand why neoliberalism came to favor capital and disfavor labor, and why it has been associated with conservative policies such as strong defense and punitive policing and prison policies, which paradoxically increase statism. In contrast, Marxists characteristically turn functionalist by arguing that neoliberalism needed the punitive state and bigger militaries. No, neoliberals reluctantly accepted these conservative policies for the sake of a politically viable alliance through which they could achieve some of their goals.

JAH: It's not a return to an old regime.

MM: Definitely not, nor simply to classical liberalism. In fact, enhanced finance capitalism is new, posing problems that had never before been confronted. Where did it come from? It came out of what are usually called neo-Keynesian policies of the postwar period. They weren't exactly Keynesian because there was a compromise between Keynesianism and general equilibrium theory, expressed for example in the Phillips curve, the supposedly inverse relation between inflation and unemployment. It's conventional to say neoliberalism emerged out of the failure of neo-Keynesianism, and there's a sense in which that is true, but it also emerged from its success in producing considerable economic development and a more prosperous society with more pensions and insurances schemes, workers paying higher tax rates, and a buoyant international economy enhancing the role of international finance.

The financialization of the economy broke through first in Britain and the US, because their economies are more international and have bigger financial centers. But then it swept through the European Union and OECD countries, and was imposed by the international banks on debt-ridden countries across the world—except for the debt-ridden United States. Thatcher and Reagan harnessed it to other conservative causes and managed to attract enough upper-working-class and lower-middle-class voters to win elections and introduce neoliberal/conservative policies. But there were different factors involved in different parts of the world, and neoliberalism didn't much change many countries. It certainly didn't bring much growth. Since the 1970s in the advanced countries growth has never reached the growth rate of the 1950s and 1960s. Together with demographic trends, this meant that states became strapped for cash. This, too, helped end the period of state expansion. In most countries—even in Britain—the size of the state now stabilized. Stabilization rather than reduction is what has generally occurred. Neoliberals have failed to reduce the size of the state. So there hasn't been a neoliberal revolution, and the degree of change has varied among different sectors and among different types of capitalism and welfare regime. Maybe now, however, the great recession brought about by neoliberalism will ironically produce state downsizing for the first time.

JAH: So it's a complicated picture. There are long-term structural changes in the economy, the breakdown of social solidarity, the revival of conservative politicians, and conservative politicians armed with a theory that is very powerful. Liberal societies are also going to face terrible problems, as increased life expectancy means that the cost of all sorts of welfare programs will be much greater than planners envisaged. So it's going to be a difficult time to run liberal states, don't you think? Promises have been made to the populations of advanced liberal states that are going to be hard to fulfill.

MM: The difficulties are going to increase.

JAH: We have spent most time talking about macro conditions. But one might argue that there are some micro factors that are missing in your account, which may produce change from the bottom up. I'm thinking of such things as demography, and I'm remembering Jack Goldstone noting that more than half the population of Egypt is probably less than fifteen years of age. Some countries have controlled population growth, but others may face the crises suggested in his model of revolution. Demography is something that happens in private life which is very different. Insurgent forces have often been denied places in university or repressed in one way or another. Demography happens in the bedroom.

MM: But such demographic forces tend to be responses to major changes elsewhere. The kinds of population growth that you're talking about have resulted from a significant improvement of infrastructures of health, on the one hand, and improvement of diet on the other. There is a period in the demographic transition before the birthrate falls, and so there is a population explosion. It's a problem in many countries now, and it can be prolonged by such things as the exclusion of women from full citizenship. That's probably got a lot to do with the Egyptian problem you mention. Now, the question is what does this crisis lead to? I think it could lead to a lot of different things. It probably means more social turbulence. In pessimistic scenarios about the future, if population growth doesn't fall quite quickly then it will interact with environmental problems and produce mass starvation and the like. You can see it in a country like Bangladesh, which is already in dire trouble. So there can be disastrous outcomes, famines and the like, but without revolution. Despite what Goldstone says, I don't see the classic revolutions actually being very closely related to demography.

JAH: Neither do I, as it happens. I was just trying to get us to think about how we might be surprised by forces which weren't there in the past, which might be in the future. The past may not be the present, and it equally might not be a good guide to the future.

There is one other thing that I've already mentioned: insofar as levels of education are going to rise, there is a great difficulty in many places because, quite often, educating the largest section of the population means that they will come to resent the minority that holds the high-level jobs, if that minority is of an ethnically different background. I think there are quite a few places in the world where the rise of the newly educated could be a major source of instability in the future.

MM: The United States has solved that by expanding credentialism. People now routinely expect to have to have a high school diploma for routine jobs, and a B.A. for any kind of job with any difficulty at all. So countries can adapt to this.

JAH: But if an ethnic marker is present, as it is in some places, the task is far from easy.

9

Contingencies of Modernity

JAH: Max Weber's work does not propose a set of sociological laws. For one thing, history could be sent down one "track" or another. For another, he stressed the importance of singular universals, that is, those evolutionary steps occurring in one place that changed the terms on which others had to operate. I have noticed in your work that there is a similar sort of viewpoint, particularly strong recently when you talked about the folly of certain geopolitical leaders. So I want to ask about the ways in which contingencies or crises might disrupt the structure of modernity. To begin with, how would you define modernity?

MM: I generally agree with Weber here. As for modernity, it is not a term I have used other than as a general referent for "in recent times." I've never been quite sure what others mean by it and I prefer not to attempt to define it. I guess you're asking about the underlying characteristics of recent and contemporary societies. I would respond by identifying capitalism in its industrial form, and the nation-state, though in a political duality with empires, plural, and then empire, singular. This triad of core structures of globalization—capitalism,

nation-states and empires—have generated class conflict, other domestic conflicts, and geopolitical conflict
over the last two hundred years. Until the 1950s this
involved the normalcy of war among states, especially
Western states. The main domestic issues have been the
extent to which the masses can participate as citizens
in the community comprised by industrial capitalism
and the nation-state, and this has involved class, gender,
and ethnic sub-issues, varying according to period and
context. The main structural tendencies have been
toward reformism and citizenship extensions domestically, and more and more deadly wars geopolitically,
until war-weariness and nuclear weapons produced
recent relative peace, except for civil wars in poorer
countries.

JAH: So the people have to enter in either as nations or as
classes, as well as citizens of liberal democracies.

MM: And the combination of industrial capitalism and the
ideal of the nation-state involve the mobilization of
the masses in one way or another. The vital question
for the early twentieth century was the way in which
this would occur, and democracy, socialism, and
fascism all offered different solutions to the entry of
the masses into the same society as elites. Since these
were alternatives, and there proved to be several ver-
sions of each, none of them can be considered to be
necessary. Democratic options combining differing
degrees of reformed capitalism, political democracy,
and social democracy / Christian democracy have been
the most successful. Not coincidentally, they are the
ones that won the hot and cold wars.

JAH: What do you mean by "not coincidentally"? Surely
the victory of these softer societies was not preordained? More important still, they might well not have
won but for the military might of the Soviet Union.

MM: By "not coincidentally" I meant that their success owed much to victory in war. But, as you say, victory in World War II owed much to the Soviet Union, which bore the brunt of the fighting against Hitler. His military power was principally ground down on the Eastern Front. The war also cemented the rule of Stalin and for a time the success of state socialism endured in peace as well as war. But it was always outweighed by the US and its allies, who had much more to offer other countries. So the victory of the "softer societies" in the Cold War, though not preordained, was always likely—provided nuclear war did not ensue.

JAH: Insofar as the outcome of war determines regimes— that is, that a different result would have given us different institutions—you are a long way from a theorist such as Gellner. Competition among states makes contingency central to your view of the world. Insofar as the United States prefers geopolitical to market dominance, this remains the case in the contemporary world.

MM: What's been characteristic of the decline of inter-state warfare is that warfare reached such a level of destruction that it became more clearly irrational to wage it, and since the US has no rival that can hurt it seriously, it remains rational for the US to use warfare as a means of geopolitics provided it does this intelligently with economic, political, and ideological supports. Of course there are still wars between lesser powers with lesser weapons, but not many of them.

JAH: So I understand why you don't like to use the concept of modernity because, in a way, contingency is built into the picture right from the start, particularly because of what happens in war. So the twentieth century was marked by enormous contingent changes. What were the main crises?

MM: So far they have been of two kinds. One is really major wars, wars more devastating than any previously known, and that's the outcome of an environment in which making war is normal. World War I happened in the same kind of ways that most wars in Europe had happened. It wasn't about empires overseas, it was about Great Powers backing up their client states in Europe.

JAH: So it was about the balance of power.

MM: Yes, a traditional war.

JAH: So why did it get so out of hand?

MM: You mean why did they fight a war that was utterly devastating? It is worth dwelling a while on this, for the processes involved were not atypical of both the major war crises of the period, and they had their analogies in both the major economic crises. They did it for somewhat irrational reasons, which is not a conventional form of causal explanation. Most explanations have a very strong element of rationality. The way I express it is that war was the default mode of diplomacy. When normal diplomatic efforts fail, war is an acceptable alternative.

The actual process by which Europe went to war in 1914 is quite complex and involves more than one set of contingencies. There was the assassination of the Archduke, which was a real coincidence. The Serbian conspirators had actually already failed in their assassination attempt, but then the Archduke's car got lost and slowly passed the café in which the disconsolate Gavrilo Princip, one of the would-be assassins, was munching a sandwich. Gavrilo seized his second chance with alacrity and killed the Archduke and his wife. There followed the resolve by the Austrian court to stand firm and punish Serbia. By a majority, the view in the Austrian court was that Austria had to fight in order to preserve its status. And ironically the death of the Archduke had lost the peace faction its leading member. This argument won out: "If we don't fight at this moment then others are going to take advantage of us too." But war would probably be against Russia too, hitherto the protector of Serbia.

Yet the Austrians were bolstered by the German government offering them military support. Indeed, the German government had decided that if it came to war it would strike not only eastward against Russia but also westward against Belgium and France. That is more puzzling, decidedly less rational. If Germany wanted its "place in the sun," it was obviously getting it anyway, peacefully. It was gradually overtaking Great Britain, industrially, economically, and acquiring hegemony on the continent. It would seem more logical to leave overseas colonies for Britain and France. They were less profitable, except for the White Dominions and India, which Germany could not get anyway. It's puzzling why the German leaders were not more patient and went instead for war. They chose war partly because they didn't believe the British would fight, and the British hadn't given them clear signals that they would fight. They couldn't do that because it was a Liberal government, and if it threatened war a third of the Liberal Cabinet would resign. There would have to be an election, and a split Liberal Party would probably lose.

As diplomacy stumbled, the mobilization of armed forces began, supposedly a defensive posture to defend oneself in case war came. But mobilization sometimes took aggressive forms. For Germany, mobilization of its armed forces actually involved occupying railheads in Belgium and Luxemburg. Belgium had treaties with France and Britain that promised they would come to the aid of Belgium if it was attacked. At this point some Germans didn't expect Britain to enter, and others did but underestimated British power and resolve. British power was a long way away: it was global, and they didn't see much of it, or anticipate the blockading power of the Royal Navy and the million-plus colonial and Dominion troops which Britain (and France) could bring to battle. Many believed British Liberal rhetoric that they were peace-loving, and thought the British didn't really have the stomach to fight or fight well. So they overestimated their chances. The Russians . . . well, I could go on like this. But the point is that the Powers could not gauge each other's reactions, and this was partly because they had different power configurations and partly because domestic motives entwined with geopolitical ones.

In all of this certain logics of geopolitics are at work, though coupled with other political and ideological logics, with contingencies added in. But what becomes obvious when these difficulties are faced up to is that there is both a readiness to go to war and relevant emotions that enter into decisions—not losing face, not backing down, in the end, "we have no choice but to show our mettle." It's like little boys in the playground fighting each other because they must show off their masculinity. There is also another underlying irrationality. In most wars all sides think they are going to win, which is the basic irrationality of war since that's not possible. Half the states lose.

JAH: I would like to add something to your account—before challenging it. The addition is simply that leaders were surprised by the destructive power of modern

techniques. They ought to have known what an industrial war was like, given that they had the examples
of the American Civil War and the Russo-Japanese
War. They failed to learn those lessons.

MM: But I think that they did know the war would be very
destructive, hence the belief that it couldn't last long.
What in fact they underestimated was their own capacity to sustain war through the mobilization of the
economy and the labor force.

JAH: And there is, it occurs to me, a further factor that is
related to this. Once you depended upon conscription,
the war had to appeal to the people: it became a war
to end all war, a war to bring democracy, and not just
a territorial dispute.

MM: To some extent. One of the curious features about
World War I is that the countries that were supposedly
aggressive, that were aggressing, didn't in the very first
place make major aggressive claims.

JAH: But they developed them.

MM: Germany made territorial claims after about three
months. So did Russia. They were defending themselves at first, but then Russian leaders began thinking
about getting to the straits of the Black Sea. As to what
they were fighting for, they all found reasons why their
own supposed national virtues were worth fighting for,
and that was the myth that sustained a degree of
popular mobilization. However, one can exaggerate
the degree of popular mobilization. These were still
hierarchal societies and people went to war essentially
because the local and national rulers told them that
this was the right thing to do and they were used to
obeying them. Of course, they developed patriotic
slogans and symbols, but the essential thing is that

they were obeying orders. It still was not an egalitarian or a democratic society.

JAH: Beyond these areas of agreement stands a difference between us. I think of the stakes of war in a slightly different way. It seems to me that in the period from the end of the nineteenth century through to 1945, the leaders of the Great Powers felt that they needed two things: nationally homogeneous societies blessed with territory, which would allow them secure sources of supply and protected markets. The crucial moment at which this changes is when France and Germany after World War II decide not to be independent in coal and steel, but to be interdependent so they don't both have separate armament industries. But before that moment Hitler's plan for geopolitical autonomy is typical. The stakes of war go up because states want to be complete power containers.

MM: Well, it would be difficult to think of Austria-Hungary in those terms, and as far as Germany is concerned, it was developing a more informal empire or hegemony over Southeastern Europe. Germany didn't need a formal empire. And the imperial rivalries were settled by diplomacy. It was not imperial rivalries that precipitated World War I. Imperial rivalries had precipitated the Russo-Japanese War of 1905. Things were different in East Asia, but that was because Japan was surrounded by other imperial powers and had few natural resources of its own. Resource imperialism was plausible for some Japanese elites and they finally won the prolonged internal debates in Japan. But I don't think that was the case for Germany or France, which did have an overseas empire. There were alternative ways of getting industrial resources, which Germany was doing anyway. The Russian were receiving lots of foreign investment so they were also satisfied on that score.

JAH: I am not quite convinced: surely what matters about economics is less the facts than what people believe the facts to be. Still, I am not saying that nationalism allied to imperialism caused war, merely that it changed the character of war once it had started.

MM: Once the war started Germany did have a greater motive for control over the continent, because once blockaded, the Germans were really in trouble. And the Austrians, too. Of course, World War II was different because one regime precipitated the conflict. The major irrationality there was the inability of Britain, France, and Russia to form a joint alliance, and that was because of ideology, the hatred between capitalism and communism.

JAH: And the exhaustion of Britain and France in World War I played a role.

MM: Yes, but their weakness had largely gone by 1938–9. It was possible that had such an alliance formed then, before Hitler had built up his massive military machine, it would have either deterred Hitler or there would have been war and Germany would have been quite quickly defeated by the combination of Britain, France, and the Soviet Union.

JAH: But this war, not just in Europe but in East Asia, too, really does unite nationalism with imperialism—even if I am wrong about the presence of this combination in World War I. Hitler really is typical, surely, in wanting *Lebensraum* for Germans together with Romanian oil so that German economic life would have continued success.

MM: Absolutely, that's what he thought he was doing. He was surprised and antagonized when Stalin wouldn't let him have dominance over Romania without war.

With the Japanese it is clear that it was a quest for empire in a traditional territorial sense.

JAH: It's an inter-imperial war which is, however, a war to the death in a way in which previous inter-imperial wars hadn't been.

MM: Partly because the means of devastation were so great, and this was also a global war: all of the continents were involved, except for Latin America.

JAH: And the national principle does start to kick in, in the sense that in several places the removal of populations is placed at the center of policy so that your national ethnicity can be dominant.

MM: And as in World War I the result is the creation of more ethnically cleansed nation-states out of empires.

So war is one type of crisis. The second type is economic, though these crises have not been as serious or as dislocating as the military crises. There have been normal cycles of growth and recession that are a part of capitalist dynamism. But the Great Depression was something else, off the scale, while our current great recession is not merely a cyclical dip. The corollary in the opposite direction was the great post-1945 boom, which of course we don't think of as a crisis. But it was also off the scale and produced major effects that are unlikely to be repeated.

JAH: And we forget moments when there are lesser depressions or recessions, which are not merely cyclical. After 1919 the return to normalcy was pretty tough in some places. In fact, throughout the 1920s few economies were very buoyant. But that led into the Great Depression, one of your major economic crises. Could you say something more about the Great Depression? What were its causes?

MM: I'll first describe its development in the US, which was the worst-affected economy. There was a sequence of shocks that cumulatively led from an ordinary recession to the Depression. We must remember that the economy of the 1920s was never very buoyant, and mass consumption was never very high. But then the mid-1920s saw a global agricultural recession caused by overproduction, the result of the Great War and its aftermath. In the US the downturn spread to construction and manufacturing in 1928. At the same time came a stock-market bubble as investors seemed overconfident in the capacity of much-touted technological progress to generate profit. The combination of overinvestment and depressed production generated massive overcapacity, bankruptcies, bank failures, and unemployment. Credit dried up and then consumption plummeted. The government and the Fed responded by deflating and restricting the money supply. This was consistent with economic orthodoxy, which held that government's role should be to only assist the "liquidation" of stock values, unprofitable businesses, excess workers and high wages—until market forces re-established equilibrium. But it didn't happen like that. Instead, such deflation turned a worsening recession into the Great Depression.

America's problems were then transmitted to an already-faltering global economy through the gold standard. Its fixed exchange rates transmitted the impact of falling prices and profits in the US to other economies. US international loans also declined, reducing foreigners' ability to export to pay for the previous loans they had received. They felt they also had to restrict credit and raise their interest rates, which meant they were also deflating during a recession.

That was the sequence of mechanisms as established by modern economists. They argue a lot about the weight of these various shocks. And they are also less good at actually explaining why such an off-the-charts depression happened when it did. To do this I think we have to broaden the explanation into industrial structure, class structure, ideology, and geopolitical rivalry—into the sources of social power more generally. For this was a more general crisis.

In very brief terms, four major structural transformations in power relations were then underway. First, agriculture, the traditional mainstay of economies, was declining, depressed because of its own global overproduction. Its travails contributed mightily to the Depression. Second, industry was transitioning through rapid technological change, from the heavy industries of the Second Industrial Revolution to lighter consumer-oriented manufacturing. Yet the combination of the two could not yet bear the weight of a full-employment economy. The old industries were no longer expanding; the new ones were still small. Technology was not yet delivering the goods. Third, the old regime class, still controlling the world's finances, was seeking to hang onto its traditional dominance by ideological adherence to "liquidationism" and the gold standard, which only made things worse. These were not just "mistakes." They were a rearguard action of class power and of a moral system. Conversely, the expanding working class seeking more social citizenship did not have the power to challenge this orthodoxy until (and only in some countries) the Depression had caused the collapse of its political allies. Fourth, there was a transition in geo-economic power away from a blend of British hegemony and coordinated policy by the Great Powers. But as yet there was not a stable replacement international regime. There was neither hegemony nor stable cooperation between the Powers since they were divided by conflicts arising from the peace treaties ending World War I.

I see support for this more structural approach to the Depression in what happened during and immediately after World War II—for the Great Depression was no more extraordinary than the equally unprecedented Great Boom that then began. This represented the coming to maturity of all four of these transitions: massive migration out of agriculture provided the labor for expanding urban-industrial sectors; an era of mass consumer industries began, linked to high consumer demand; universal social citizenship in welfare benefits, progressive taxes, and policy commitment to full employment and high wages was institutionalized; and the United States, the new hegemon, supplied workable rules for the international economy. The comparison reveals, of course, that economies are always entwined with the other sources of social power, in good times as well as bad.

JH: You mentioned at the start that finance has much greater importance in contemporary capitalism. Does that make the crisis of 2007–8 wholly different from the Great Depression?

MM: There were both similarities and differences. Both were precipitated by financial crises, being preceded by credit-fueled bubbles and worsened by a debt crisis. Both came after a period of rising inequality and sagging mass incomes, and both came after a period of technological ingenuity that failed to generate much growth. Though the financial services sector is now much bigger than it was in the interwar period, then they were the core of the ruling class of the time, the "old regime," and political economy was tailored to their needs. As I have just indicated, governments bound themselves to the fetters of the gold standard in order to demonstrate to investors the "soundness" of their economies. In both crises financial speculators were being appeased.

But yes, the debt level today is vastly greater than in the Great Depression. There was no equivalent then of the global imbalances that piled debts so high yet seemed to offer an easy solution of debt to sagging incomes. The very visible fetters of the gold standard have yielded to the less visible fetters of a floating dollar and transnational capital. Little regulation had existed before the Great Depression, whereas this recession has followed considerable regulation followed by deregulation. The response in the 1930s was greater domestic regulation but beggar-thy-neighbor devaluation and protectionism internationally. Today there is more of a balance between international and domestic regulation. The difference is that most countries today have been through a lengthy period of greater state involvement in economic life, involving prioritizing industry over finance, unemployment over inflation, Keynesianism over neoclassical economics, and with the presence of substantial welfare states. Most recently, neoliberalism has sought to kick back against this, and it has made some headway, especially in the Anglophone countries.

Yet considerable variations in political economy remain, much greater than those among advanced economies when the Great Depression hit. Perhaps when talking earlier about the current crisis I did not stress enough these variations. The Nordic countries and the bigger and more stable European economies, like France and Germany, are much less intrinsically vulnerable to speculation than is the UK or the countries of southern Europe. It is because of the peculiarities of their sharing the euro that they have seemed to be in the same vulnerable boat. Japan, India, and China are even less vulnerable, while Australia benefits from its trade with China, Canada benefits from having very strong regulation of its financial sector, and the US benefits from having the world's reserve currency. Despite greater globalization now, there is also more national variability in political economy, which indicates once again that globalization involves the globalization of the nation-state.

JH: How might we prioritize the causes of the recent crisis? Many factors were present—"animal spirits" in Wall Street and the failure of key executives to understand new financial tools among them—but I suspect that two elements matter enormously. The first is the sheer amount of liquidity in the world economy, in large part resulting from savings in East Asia. This is the issue of "global imbalances," which created the possibility of a housing boom in the United States. Second, in the United States a desperately unequal government sought to buy social peace by pushing cheap mortgages because it is so difficult in that country to redistribute income through other means.

MM: This is right on the nail as far as the subprime mortgage contribution to the crisis, which did provide the tipping mechanism into actual crisis. The conservative-neoliberal offensive in the United States lasting from Ronald Reagan to Bush the Younger greatly increased inequality. The household incomes of most Americans stagnated over the whole period, while the rich got much richer. Then, at the other end of the earth, the growth of Japan, then China, supplemented by the oil revenues of Middle Eastern states, produced large export surpluses for them and the holding of massive quantities of dollars. They were invested in the United States, which lowered interest rates and generated massive amounts of cheap available credit. Ordinary American families could borrow to finance a more prosperous lifestyle. They used their houses as ATMs to finance the American Way of Life. Even the poor were offered subprime mortgages. Unfortunately for them, the mortgages were at variable interest rates.

At the first sign of overheating the Fed raised interest rates in 2005 and the poor could not make their repayments. Their "toxic" debts had by now been hidden among larger packages of debt obligations, contaminating them, and the crisis began. I would just add that the mortgage debts were only a small part of the proliferation of overall debt, and that even without subprime mortgages there would have been a similar crisis further down the track. The financial services sector was out of control.

JH: A final question on this issue: has the US come out Afairly well from the crisis, while the supposedly more regulated European economies have possibly come out less well?

MM: It is more complicated than that. Actually, the Europeans also deregulated finance capital in the sense of removing capital controls as completely and only slightly later than the Anglophones. But the countries of the Eurozone also have an additional unregulated hole: they share a common currency but no common Treasury determining overall fiscal policy. The European Central Bank has only very limited powers, and so, for example, there is no automatic authority to steer subsidies to depressed member countries such as Greece. Individual nation-states can do this. The British Treasury can do this for Northern Ireland; the American Treasury can do it for West Kentucky. In this respect the Europeans are less regulated than the Anglophones, and they share a common vulnerability as a result. However, in other ways they are much more "regulated." Their bigger welfare states, for example, can cushion living standards and consumer demand, so that rising unemployment does not produce for them a deflationary effect comparable to that of the Anglos. The stability of the euro is very difficult to predict, but in other respects the continental

Europeans are likely to come out of crisis better than the British and Americans because of their more interventionist states.

JH: I would now like to ask you about potential crises in the world today. So let us return to China for a moment. It has the possibility of developing now, more or less in tandem with the United States. Is this situation stable?

MM: Well, anything is possible, but I don't think serious trouble is likely. China has major decisions to make. It would be better for the Chinese people if there were more domestic development, and if a greater proportion of Chinese resources was put into domestic infrastructures, especially in the rural areas and especially to reduce the very high current level of inequality, and to produce a more balanced economy domestically and internationally, reducing global imbalances. I don't think that China will be beset by social disorder that would simply prevent it from doing this. I think the regime has a choice. If they really tried to do this, it would be doable and a benefit for China and the rest of the world. That would be a very healthy development, though we cannot be sure it will actually happen.

JAH: Bits of information that come out from meetings of American Treasury secretaries with Chinese officials give the impression that Chinese leaders are very clever. They don't want to pull the rug out from underneath the dollar by getting rid of a huge surplus, because if they sent the American economy into a tailspin they would be hurting themselves. Why cause a crisis in the world economy that would hurt you? They seem to know this.

MM: The most obvious problem for them is that withdrawal would devalue their holdings in the United

States. They would lose a lot of money in the process. I guess they will seek to diversify, but they will do it slowly.

JAH: Yes, and possibly if the nice scenario came true, they would put some of the savings into internal development, therefore domestic demand, therefore more balance. So there's no crisis there.

MM: And that also helps the development of the rest of Asia: being able to sell more to China, being able to receive more from China. Of course we mustn't forget India here, which doesn't contribute nearly as much to these global imbalances, but would also play a larger role in the global economy as it developed. So I think that it would be feasible that a global economy can be developed that is more multicentered and which exists on a greater level of interdependence than has ever happened before. That's not where the crisis will come from.

JAH: So are there other dangerous points where crises might develop?

MM: Well, at the lower level, they are less crises than problems, varying around the world. Some of them are local crises. Ethnic conflict and ethnic cleansing will continue to exist in some countries. There's no quick and easy solution to those problems, but ethnic cleansing is making its way through the world and nowadays it doesn't affect many of the biggest societies. The biggest ones that have had touches of it, India and Indonesia, have developed ways of handling it that keep it at quite a low level.

The Europeans and Japanese have a different though related problem: immigration. They will have to cope with continued levels of immigration, partly because these countries are failing to reproduce themselves demographically. That problem could get more serious and produce a rightwing backlash. It could produce a resurgence of not fascism but nativism. Then there is the problem of the contemporary state, given escalating costs and static or falling revenues, a lower proportion of the economically active compared to the inactive, and the reluctance of citizens to pay higher taxes. That creates a fiscal crisis for the state that is likely to worsen. We're now talking about lesser problems, not catastrophes. The specific problem for political parties is that they are likely to go in and out of government if they fail to solve these problems.

JAH: But that is not going to change the character of the social system.

MM: Probably not. But there is one major crisis looming. It's highly ironic that everything that is counted as an economic triumph in the twentieth century has produced a major dark side: damage to the environment. GDP and GDP per capita are universally regarded as symbols of success and of beneficence. But they are positively correlated with environmental degradation, of which the key aspect is climate change occurring on a global scale—global warming is the popular expression.

10

Our Looming Crisis

JAH: Your claim that damage to the environment might cause genuine catastrophe, and the related insistence that environmentalism may become a total ideology, deserves sustained consideration. This seems to me to be a tremendously important question for a rather more mundane reason: social peace inside advanced capitalist societies has often been maintained by growth. The fact that the pie gets bigger means that people at the bottom of society are relatively content because their standard of living is going up even though their piece of the pie isn't necessarily getting larger. To imagine a world in which this mechanism for securing peace might disappear terrifies me. But let me put my own fear to one side for a moment so as to ask for your view of the nature of the crisis?

MM: Well, of course I have no expertise at all in the science part of it. I have to take for granted what is now the overwhelming consensus among climate scientists: that climate change is occurring and that it is largely anthropogenic—caused by human activity. Thus human behavior must be changed in order to mitigate the effects of climate change. They key index is emissions of carbon dioxide, which contribute over 70 percent of all the greenhouse gases. Such emissions must be greatly reduced if human societies are to remain healthy. We then add the projections of economists about the likely costs and effects of different policies. Here there is an enormous amount of guesswork, so that the most careful work always gives a range of possible variations and it qualifies its conclusions in terms of level of probability. You can't be precise at all. Nobody has any real idea of how quickly or radically we have to act. But we clearly must act and it is better to be safe than sorry, if, as seems highly likely, the failure to act would bring disaster perhaps on our grandchildren, perhaps on their children.

The problem is, of course, that action must be global or near-global. Unless the United States, Europe, and the BRIC countries at a minimum took very similar actions of effective mitigation, it is unlikely disaster could be averted. This is the most global crisis ever because any emission of carbon dioxide anywhere in the world contributes to the warming of the entire planet, and therefore affects every country in the world, at least to a small degree. The problem is that this requires a higher level of international agreement than has ever existed. Any solution has to come through massive amounts of international negotiation and agreement. That's the first problem.

The second international problem is that there has emerged a fundamental disagreement, based on self-interest, between richer nations and poorer nations. About 70 percent of the existing level of carbon dioxide in the atmosphere has been produced by the advanced countries in the past 100 years. But an increasing portion is now being contributed by the poorer nations, and if they are to industrialize, and that was always believed to be a good thing for them to do, and we were supposedly helping them to do this, then their level of emissions would increase per capita beyond ours. At the moment the divide is somewhat artificial, since we in the North have exported many of our high-polluting manufacturing industries to them, and then we import back the relatively clean finished products. We have given them our pollution. But if they do raise their own living standards by consuming industrial products themselves, then they will pollute even more.

JAH: At that stage it would overtake that of the advanced capitalist world. The US is contributing perhaps 25 percent of global emissions, but China is getting close. But if a billion people in China had a car—and there is no moral reason why they shouldn't have what we possess—then there would be catastrophic damage to the environment. And here we come to questions of political economy. The United States is calling for China to raise its standards of consumption, so as to deal with the problem of global imbalances; but to solve that problem would lead to an increase in dangers for the environment.

MM: That is true. Though global imbalances were not the sole cause of the current great recession, they certainly contributed. It is highly ironic that the obvious way to reduce them would be for the Chinese to invest more within China itself, to build up the country's infrastructures and to encourage domestic consumption. This would result—indeed, it is already beginning to result—in more energy-intensive and polluting industries like cement, iron, and steel, and coal to power them. This hastens climate change. Unfortunately, Chinese economic growth outweighs all the improvements they are making to energy efficiency. This makes ever more urgent the task of finding international agreements that can overcome this North/South divide.

Then we have almost every country's main domestic problem, which is that their economies are overwhelmingly capitalist, based on the legitimacy of private profit. Environmentalists call it the "treadmill" of profit. Most of the problem lies with particular major emitting industries, above all the energy industry itself, the producers of coal, oil and natural gas and electricity, and its major consumers. Any policy would have to involve serious penalties for those industries: serious sanctions against them for emitting so much carbon dioxide, almost certainly leavened by incentives for them to stop and shift toward renewable energy. That's very difficult because these are major industries that governments typically want to protect because they are an important part of the domestic economy. Governments want other countries to constrain their industries, but freedom for their own. Some business has been shifting somewhat and there are now many corporations with green policies, but they tend not to be the biggest polluters, and the biggest polluters are mainly shifting only in token ways. There are political systems in which they have a great deal of power, one of them being the American political system.

The problem also lies with ourselves, as consumers, who love automobile and airline travel, air conditioning and heated swimming pools. It's true that public opinion polls have shown a steady increase during the twenty-first century in the proportions of people concerned about climate change and wishing to take steps to mitigate it. This has persuaded most political parties to adopt green-sounding rhetoric. But as a political issue it seems to be of low salience and its salience has declined during the great recession. Most people still want to improve GDP and reduce the unemployment rate more than they want to reduce greenhouse gas emissions. Politicians realize this and lower their green profile.

The unequal production of greenhouse gases is produced domestically as well as internationally. The average citizen of Wyoming produces ten times as many emissions as those of California, which means that you have to persuade the citizens of Wyoming to shift their patterns more than you do the citizens of California. You also need to penalize the industries of Wyoming. In this case we are mainly talking about coal. It's not just a problem of the coal industry providing corrupting subsidies to congressmen and senators, it's also the congressmen and senators from such states protecting the interests of their own constituents. So all of the normal problems of political life, cast onto a global stage, have to be overcome for there to be serious progress.

At the moment, progress has obviously been minimal. But at the same time, you can look at it another way. You could say, well, it's actually been quite substantial progress because it's only been thirty years since there was serious consciousness of these issues. That's not a long time. In that thirty-year period, the scientists have also firmed up their consensus, and in principle most political leaders have been convinced that some action is necessary. So you might say that it's quite a lot of progress, though it is clear that it does not even keep pace with the growth of emissions, whose level keeps on increasing.

One special problem has been that this has been arising in a period dominated, especially in the US, by neoliberalism, which opposes state intervention in principle. Yet it is coordinated state intervention that becomes ever more urgent, and so ideologies of free markets must be also combated. It adds up to a really formidable task.

JAH: I take the point about the internal political–economic constraints upon solutions. But if you think about the more general North–South divide it is impossible to imagine a solution that involves redistribution on a world scale. You can't imagine American politicians allowing for a fall in living standards to transfer potential for other countries to develop—at least I can't imagine that. I think national interests are too strong. So any solution would have to involve some possibility of continuing growth and increasing living standards. Environmentalists who would like us to live a simpler life are not likely to produce any plan that would be politically accepted.

MM: Well, the conservative business-friendly solution—by those who accept that the problem exists—is faith in our technological ability. There is more investment in R & D in new technologies, either from the government or by giving incentive to business by giving them tax breaks. "Clean coal," for example, would allow the coal industry and the citizens of Wyoming to continue business as usual. There's no such thing as clean coal at the moment. It's a fraud perpetrated by the mining industry, as Al Gore goes round the world saying. There is a possible future technique, "carbon capture and storage," where the carbon from coal is captured and stored in massive underground silos. But at present it's only a theory, not even a working model. The rival fusion reactor projects in France, California, and England will supposedly produce totally clean and renewable energy, but are not yet off the drawing board either.

JAH: I agree that it is very worrying. But it is an important question because so much of Chinese development, as I understand it, comes from the use of really filthy coal. There's no sign of fusion power on the horizon.

MM: No. Wind and solar have a certain contribution to make but it will be nowhere near enough. It looks as if nuclear power has to be a part of it.

JAH: Conservative people, including me, pray for scientific breakthroughs given the difficulty of imagining a world without growth. But "cap and trade" is pretty conservative as well.

MM: That's not so conservative as reliance on technological innovation. It is the next step up in policy activism. Cap and trade works by setting an overall cap on emissions and issuing emissions credits to businesses. Businesses that do not reach that cap are allowed to sell their remaining credits to those that wish to exceed the cap. It's a series of financial incentives and disincentives. How tough this is depends initially on the overall level set for the cap and then on how quickly the cap is reduced in successive years. In theory it could be a radical rather than a conservative policy, but since existing schemes are only put in place after protracted negotiations with business, they tend to not be tough enough to make much of a difference. Sometimes they can even result in an increase in emissions. European Union schemes have tended to get a little tougher through time, but many environmentalists decry these schemes as inadequate.

Normally considered more radical is direct state regulation, states dictating what level of emissions is allowable in each country, according to standards set by international agreements . . .

JAH: Through a Kyoto-type protocol?

MM: Yes, and then sector by sector. The state gives targets and fines heavily those who don't meet them. Again, however, existing schemes are rather puny. Both types of scheme do usually tend to reduce emissions, but not nearly enough to offset the general effect of economic development through the world. So aggregate emissions keep on rising. Unlike most environmentalists, I don't see a clear distinction between cap and trade, which is usually seen as being necessarily business-friendly, versus state regulation, which is by fiat, because either could be either too lenient or tough enough to do the job. But the latter would involve coercion of business—and of consumers too.

JAH: Suggested changes to cap and trade legislation don't seem very radical at the moment—and there are all sorts of tricks, like shunting your dirty industries offshore.

MM: Yes, but some of these can have a positive effect. For example, forests have the capacity to absorb much of our carbon emissions, so deforestation is a major threat, contributing about 20 percent of all greenhouse gas emissions in the 1990s. The Intergovernmental Panel on Climate Control in its Fourth Assessment Report concluded that reducing or preventing deforestation is the policy option with the largest and most immediate impact on carbon levels. If we can shovel enough funds into Indonesia, Brazil, and a handful of other countries to persuade them to radically cut their deforestation below their level of replanting, that would be a significant step toward cutting emissions. Since it is unlikely, as you observed, that we would simply subsidize them, international cap-and-trade programs have appeared instead, in which poor countries can sell their emissions credits to dirty industry in the North, and the money for that would be tied to investment in new technology projects in poorer countries. Again, of course, it depends on how big and tough the scheme is and how focused it is on the worst emissions. It is possible to tackle the worst and most easily remediable emissions and in the process allow lesser emitters to flourish. But again, so far little progress has been made.

However, the overall politics involved to implement any effective programs are so difficult that it seems most likely that there will not be a steady, agreed reduction of carbon emissions on the scale sufficient to ward off disaster. It's more likely that we will get to some kind of tipping-point that generates a real crisis . . .

JAH: A crisis would come in what form? Flooding?

MM: Yes, that's the likeliest. The total flooding of low-lying small island states, or general flooding of a country like Bangladesh.

JAH: A major, truly irreversible humanitarian disaster.

MM: Yes, and one that was obviously related to global warming, to greenhouse gas emissions. At that point we would hope that the scientific establishment would act collectively, speak with one voice, and have a big impact on the world's media, and then on the mass public and politicians. There could be a more serious set of policies born out of necessity. This is the relatively optimistic scenario.

JAH: You are relying on necessity becoming the mother of invention.

MM: Exactly, but a more pessimistic scenario is that there would be a massive popular reaction to the floods which forced governments into a serious relief operation, helping out refugees, feeding them, and perhaps even resettling them elsewhere. The governments would announce that when the refugee crisis was over, they would collectively turn to long-term solutions— but when the crisis died out of the news, replaced by a child molestation or corruption scandal, they would forget about it until the next crisis. It is also an unfortunate fact that global warming does not affect everybody equally. It is highly likely to affect poorer countries worse. Canada and the northern US states might even benefit from a five-degree warming. In any case, the richer countries have far more resources to protect their own territories. Look at the Netherlands, much of which would be underwater if governments over hundreds of years had not spent massive sums on dykes.

So countries might not all have equal incentive. A disaster in Bangladesh might product humanitarian relief programs, but not the requisite political changes, because the citizens of the United States or of Northern Europe would not be sufficiently motivated. Now if we went along that path, it might lead toward massive refugee flows, possible wars over water resources, and various other kinds of intense conflict, including international terrorism, on a scale comparable to world war, but more chaotic.

JAH: We obviously have to think about all this, but in a way these issues are too appalling to contemplate.

MM: Yes, but one thing I do know from personal experience is that right now the intelligence services of the major Powers are playing scenario games about the alternative policy options for them resulting from such disaster. The CIA is gaming events such as a Bangladesh disaster.

JAH: I pray for technological progress because I cannot see a way in which a political will can be created to deal with environmental crises unless there is some way of continuing growth within the world economy.

MM: Well, most environmental scientists and economists say that we have alternatives, and that continuing climate change will produce bigger negative effects on GDP than the costs of alternative energy programs. That's the claim that they make, and at some point that's going to be true. But the time horizons of most people are short, as economists note when discussing the "discounting" of future costs. They rate costs incurred now much higher than savings supposedly made decades down the line. And since disaster is unlikely in the short run, paying higher taxes now to subsidize immediate emissions policies is not likely to be popular. The problem is that the threat is much too abstract and long-run. It doesn't bite at peoples' every-day lives, yet.

JAH: The Copenhagen meeting was, in this regard, pro-foundly depressing.

MM: Yes. The US, China, and some others essentially sabo-taged it, in the process deliberately undermining the European Union's pretensions to leadership on climate change. Great-Power games are being played.

JAH: There is no moral reason why Chinese peasants in the countryside should not have a decent standard of living, but the Chinese proposals presented in Copen-hagen allowing that meant that no solution was envis-aged to environmental problems.

MM: Of course, yet the Chinese government has shifted its position over the last decade, and politics in China are very different, so the Communist Party has no prob-lems in having to convince industry or anything like that. If the Central Committee of the Party makes the decision, then that's that.

JAH: But Chinese political stability depends upon providing a growing economy. So it's a question of having dif-ferent sources of energy to do it.

MM: Yes, but the advantage of China is that its leadership has a longer time frame than almost any other country in the world, and so it can more easily conceive of the need to make substantial reductions in the medium term. In fact, I'm relatively optimistic about China. Its extraordinary growth rate might bring extraordinary pollution, but it also gives the government resources to finance alternative energy policy. As you say, continued industrialization will obviously increase carbon emissions in China by a significant amount, whatever they do now. But I think that the leadership has become aware of this problem, has a longer time frame, and can potentially do something about it.

I'm more pessimistic about the United States, partly because of short political time horizons, the stalemated political system and know-nothing anti-science opposition within the Republican Party. The Waxman/Markey Emissions Bill was greatly watered down to get it passed through the House but there is currently no timetable to present it in the Senate because Republicans won't agree to it, nor indeed will Democrats who represent high emissions states. So for the Obama administration, which does genuinely care about climate change, this bill has sunk well below other issues such as health care and banking reform in its list of priorities. Again, the issue is too abstract to win elections. The US is now lagging behind the EU, whereas in the 1970s the US led on environmental issues. And I see no prospect for changing this. As the Republicans won the November elections, the prospects have worsened further. I am pessimistic.

JAH: I begin to see why you see this as *the* potential crisis of the twenty-first century, like no other.

MM: This is a very different crisis to anything that we've experienced before. The earlier crises loomed quite suddenly and unexpectedly, and they overwhelmed the diplomatic and economic institutions that were supposed to cope. The twentieth-century experience of crises is in fact largely one of failure. But we now perceive not only that global climate change has been a long-term process over the whole of the industrial period, but also that it is going to steadily intensify over the next half-century. It is unique for scientists and social scientists to be able to confidently predict long-term future changes, in this case bringing disaster on an unprecedented scale, both intensively and extensively. Thereafter, if mitigation was not successful, there would probably occur a series of fairly sudden tipping-points, of great natural but man-made disasters. And all this is predictable, within normal statistical significance levels, well in advance. If rationality was a primary human attribute, it would be a no-brainer. But reason does not dominate collective decision-making. We could be as helpless as the dinosaurs!

It is also the only crisis that results directly from human success through the world. That is another reason it is so hard to take mitigating action. The terrible irony of it is that it's our very success at increasing collective economic power that might well destroy us. At the height of this civilization's power, when it seems that economic growth can be spread to the world, the rug is pulled from under it.

JAH: Just at a moment when some of the crises to do with war are understood better, just at this moment of success, everything looks as if it could go wrong in a new way.

MM: That's right. It is a characteristic of the drive to economic growth in the industrial period. It is not just capitalism. In our countries it is indeed the drive for profit that is the mechanism, the treadmill, of disaster, but that wasn't the case in the Soviet Union or China, where the mechanism was and is state commitment to higher growth—indeed, growth became synonymous for the Soviet regime with socialism. Nobody has produced adequate figures on whether capitalism or state socialism did more damage to the environment, but any difference cannot have been great.

To solve it, of course, does need a much higher level of state regulation than we've been talking about in relation to the financial crisis or even the Great Depression, and it's interesting that there are economic sociologists who take what they see as a Polanyian line that capitalism has cyclical tendencies oscillating between state and market. But it's not really quite like that because each phase in which there has been or needs to be greater regulation has specific and usually broader causes. They are rather different to the previous one. In the Great Depression, the regulation was needed as a response to the economic tendencies and class conflict of capitalism, linked to unstable geopolitical relations. The extension of regulation after World War II was due to the boost it was given by the war. The neoliberal reaction from the 1970s was due not only to inherent problems of neo-Keynesianism but also to weakening labor movements, a conservative revival, and a swing in power toward the United States. Now the boost to state regulation that should happen (whether it does happen is another matter) comes from a wholly unexpected source, the very success of the capitalist and state socialist systems. And it's not just that markets need more regulation, but that our entire set of social practices need it. We consumers need to mitigate our behavior too.

JAH: So maybe your final volume should have "the environment" in the title.

MM: I haven't settled on the title yet, but it will contain the word "crisis" or "crises."

JAH: So just when you've explained all the previous crises you've thought of a new one!

MM: Yes. The counter-movement is also novel. The opposition is a new combination of science and environmental NGOs and "green" people. Ralph Schroeder has always urged me to add science as a separate source of power.

JAH: He has a bit of a point.

MM: Yes. I've always resisted it on the notion that science is "cold" and rational, and that scientists, by and large, were servants of power, usually of entrepreneurs, militaries, or states. But as this crisis looms, we see the emergence of a corporate body of scientists taking stances that differ significantly from those of its supposed "masters," and persuading some of those masters to embrace their position. This body of scientists is in a quasi-alliance with a bunch of NGOs, some of them anarchists and ecoterrorists, others comprising a whole range of organizations from Greenpeace to animal and bird societies. Science seems to be becoming a little less "cold," tolerating a more emotional-ideological set of allies. Of course, historians of science such as Margaret Jacobs have shown us that early modern science, personified by Newton, emerged out of religion. In that period science was "warm." The present "warm" combination of scientists and environmentalists, which "green" movements have mobilized quite well, is currently persuading people that in their everyday lives they can make a difference by recycling, buying fuel-efficient cars, and the like.

JAH: All those are good things. There is also the innovative idea of Fred Hirsch, arguing that instead of giving people with the inherently most interesting jobs the highest salaries, you might be able to install a little bit of social peace by cutting the salaries of the most interesting jobs, because those positions will be filled anyway because of their intrinsic interest. In other words, disconnect status and emolument. It might be very hard to put this into practice!

MM: Well, that simply ignores the distribution of power in society, which is dominated by those with interesting jobs. But the environmental movement has, in quite a short space of time, achieved a surprising popularity. What it can't do, as yet, is to shift the reality of political power when it gets down to the nitty gritty of policy. Some steps are taken, but not enough.

JAH: And it's a very divided movement in that some of the people, just as you said, are wanting new technologies so that growth can be there, but there are the morally admirable people who wish to cut down on our carbon footprint and live simpler lives, and are prepared to try and envision the world without so much economic growth. Social movements that don't have core cohesion can often fracture.

MM: Yes, though some aspects of that can be seen as a strength rather than a weakness. The fact that it's diverse means that a lot of different types of energy can be pushed in a similar direction. Also, you find that at the international conferences such as Copenhagen the major environmental NGOs do not have an official status, but they are accredited to be there, they can sit on panels, they produce literature, they produce a daily newspaper about what happened on each day, which most state delegates don't know. Their activities are quite impressive, but they have a long way to go before they can convince people to make sacrifices. Moreover, at the inter-governmental conferences, big business has a more privileged insider access to national delegations than do the NGOs. That would need to change.

JAH: Yes, or it will be necessary to find some way with new technologies. But I want to close this particular discussion by asking you about the recent revival of neoliberalism or marketism. Does that mean that solutions to the environmental crisis are less likely than ever?

MM: Yes, unfortunately. The environmental crisis could not be coming at a worse time. The rise of neoliberalism is a disaster for coping with climate change for two reasons. First, it asserts that markets can solve everything. Whatever the truth of this proposition in other contexts, in climate change it is simply false. Present market forces need heavy steering to ward off disaster. Second, neoliberalism has led to a downward economic spiral, first stagnation, then finance-induced recession, then sovereign debt issues responded to with deflation, and so probably to further recession. This is not a context in which environmentalists can make much headway. Politicians want to protect jobs and profits above all else. They will not finance new projects in alternative energies that might produce jobs or profits some years down the track.

These two neoliberal obstacles are the reason that cap-and-trade policies are being sold—and denounced by radical environmentalists—as market-friendly. But as I have said, it depends entirely on the level of the cap and its subsequent tightening as to whether it is market-friendly. The only policies that would be market-friendly, that is, business-friendly, would be ineffective ones. And that is what is being proposed—and barely even implemented.

So we may have to get out of this neoliberal rut before we can address climate change, which makes it even likelier that a tipping-point generating an environmental disaster would be necessary before serious action was taken. Progress, development, evolution, all those temptations of a fundamentally optimistic cast of thought since the Enlightenment, might be at an end.

Conclusion

JAH: I want to end these interviews by returning to your theoretical model, so as to allow you to reflect upon its efficacy. Let me begin critically. As your book has moved closer to our own times it has sometimes become less clear. Power sources are seen to intermingle, a process that you have characterized as "polymorphously perverse." Are you worried by that? More important, is it the case that your model occasionally allows you to sit on the fence, so to speak, adding factors rather than truly explaining which one is dominant?

MM: I characterize this problem as the Engels/Weber debate. As the first true follower of Marx, Engels declared that societies were characterized by a whole host of causal interconnections, but finally, "in the last instance," economic relations would assert themselves as ultimately necessary and primary. In contrast Max Weber said that no overall generalizations could be made about the relations between what he called the structures of social action. You characterize me as siding with Weber on this issue, but my position is more nuanced than this. I have steered my own path somewhere between the two, in five distinct respects.

First, from the beginning of *The Sources of Social Power*, I have identified not one but four principal power sources. Thus my argument, unlike Weber's, is that in the last instance societies can be explained by the interactions of these four, and does not require myriad other causes as well. Of course, I am too much of an empiricist to make this an inviolable principle, a law. Societies and human beings are almost infinitely variable, and the world remains very large. Human experiences remain diverse. In the warlike twentieth century, many millions of people were deeply disrupted and damaged by war, yet many more millions remained largely untouched by it. Nonetheless, these four sources of social power do the theoretical spadework for my "theories of the middle range," as C. Wright Mills termed generalizations about overall social development.

Second, I offer theories of the middle range about the relations between the four power sources which are specific to the "leading edge" of power in particular historical eras. In Volume I, for example, I argued that during the era of ancient empires, military power relations attained alongside economic power relations a primacy in the structuring of societies. Then followed an era of world religions in which ideological power relations became primary structures. In Volume II, I suggested that in the first part of its period, from 1760 to 1815, entwined economic and military power relations were primary, followed by a period up to 1914 when political power in the shape of the rising national state replaced military power in this duo—though I now see that that conclusion neglected the role of empires.

In Volume III, concerning the period from World War I up to today, I argue that economic power in the shape of capitalism and political power in the shape of the nation-state (qualified by the persistence of American Empire) have become the most causally powerful. I also suggest that if humanity is to overcome the problem of climate change, it has to reduce the power of both capitalism and the nation-state. Whether this will happen is another matter, of course. Power, not efficiency, rules the world—more exactly, distributive power dominates collective power. But I do not believe that one can have one theory of ultimate primacy for the whole historical development of society or for the whole world at any single point in time.

However, third, I do allow for the possibility in the future of two alternative, extreme "last instances." One is a new version of Engels's economic primacy. Climate change is now caused by capitalist profit-seeking, by state support to capitalism, and by our excessive consumption of commodities (this combination is more statist, less capitalist in China). If those capitalist forces are not reined in by aggressive national and international policies, then economic power—capitalism—will have destroyed the planet, which would definitely be a "last instance" for humanity. The other possible last instance is military, the onset of nuclear war, or war fought with other weapons of mass destruction, which would have the same destructive result. That would end civilized human societies. But failing such extremes, there is no last instance.

Fourth, I offer generalizations about the overall nature of each power source. Economic power provides the most stably integrated and most steadily developing intensive and extensive set of power relations. Globalizing production and trade networks have provided extensive economic power relations over more and more of the world; while production relations provide intensive controls over our everyday lives. The combination ensures that economic power is the most securely and persistently implanted in everyday life, almost throughout the globe, and its development is the most persistent. Military power relations have provided the most destructive power, almost always in short, sharp bursts, destabilizing societies, accelerating some social changes, slowing others, and occasionally directing them down new paths.

But military power relations changed greatly in the nineteenth and twentieth centuries, as their massively increasing destructive power began to outweigh by far any capacity to reconstruct. These reconstructing abilities had been much greater in earlier empires and after earlier wars. Ideological power relations also exercise their greatest force in short, sharp bursts, when crises generated by the other power sources overwhelm existing institutions, and new movements emerge, flourishing plausible, total, and often utopian alternative solutions with a high emotional content and an unrivalled capacity to distinguish between supposedly "good" and "evil" social practices. Finally, political power relations channel and institutionalize the other power sources over definite bounded territories, giving an overall spatial stability to social life. In the contemporary world nation-states have penetrated into the heart of capitalism, giving it the two dialectics, national/transnational and international/transnational, which define the overall process of globalization (along with the third element of American Empire).

Fifth, my power sources offer a normative theory of pluralism, that is, of a more genuinely democratic society in which overall power would neither be concentrated in a single source of power, nor in a single elite controlling all sources. Instead, power should be balanced between groups wielding economic, ideological, and political power. This is developed in Volume III in my critiques of both the Soviet Union (an example of the single party-state elite) and the United States (an example of the encroachment by economic on political and ideological power).

This seems to me to be a not inconsiderable set of responses to your criticism.

JAH: If you look back over your whole project, do you feel that your approach has been successful, that you have been able to tell us things that we might have missed so that we can see the world in a new way? More specifically, to what extent do you draw on previous theorists such as Marx, Wallerstein, or Hobsbawm, for example? And what is original about your view of the long twentieth century?

MM: I think that I have given sufficient detail in our conversations of my approach for readers to draw their own conclusions as to whether they can learn anything from me. My long twentieth century, from 1914 to 2010, is arbitrary in its end date, which is today. But it is integrated by a series of major crises, from World War I to climate change, which punctuate the whole period, in which we can judge causes, human responses and outcomes. They also raise major problems of causation: the extent to which we can explain the conjunctures of secular, structural tendencies and the single shattering event. Most views of the twentieth century dichotomize it between the first half-century characterized by disaster and the second half characterized by recovery, golden age, and the problems of abundance—from Holocaust to teenagers out of control. My view is different. Crises are endemic to human societies; they are the inevitable but unintended consequences of action by the most creative species on our planet.

As to influences, clearly, my writing on capitalism draws freely from Marx and his followers, but I am a social democrat and a pluralist, not a Marxist. Though I appreciate the writings of recent Marxists like Immanuel Wallerstein or Giovanni Arrighi or David Harvey, I find them to be ultimately reductionist and functionalist. They reduce other sources of social power to playing functional roles for the development of the capitalist mode of production, which they see as being systemic, as ultimately defining social structure as a whole. I argued against seeing societies as social systems in the first chapter of Volume I, and I have not changed my mind since. Arrighi did add geopolitical power relations to capitalism in his model of successive imperial hegemonies, but I find that too systemic as well. Harvey distinguished (as I do) between territorial and market aspects of imperialism in order to analyze the American Empire, but he only actually used the latter in his empirical analysis, which is reductionist. Others in the Marxian tradition have shown a lighter touch. Eric Hobsbawm in his recent writings has shown a full appreciation of nations, alongside classes. Robert Brenner maintains a systemic view of capitalism while not claiming that it determines other power sources—we are agreed that the Iraq War cannot be reduced to economic causes, for example. And Perry Anderson writes with great insight on everything, wearing his Marxism lightly, and appreciating a great diversity of theory.

I generally move right away from Marxists when dealing with ideological, military, and political power relations, all of which they neglect or reduce. Yet most other "schools" of contemporary theory are not all that interesting. Rational choice theory is inappropriate to most of the major trends of the twentieth century, since human beings have repeatedly shown themselves to be ideological, emotional, and irrational. In your biography of Ernest Gellner, you quote him saying, "A genuine commitment to rationality means that one must admit that it is poorly grounded." Exactly! Cultural theory should have more to say about the specificities of ideological power than it does, but unfortunately it tends to see culture everywhere, enveloping all, and so has largely abandoned any specific explanatory power, any causal role, for culture or ideology when set against the other sources of social power. Political sociologists in their reaction against class theories have greatly exaggerated the role of institutions, while theories of globalization tend to be economistic, overenthusiastic, or vacuous.

But empirically informed theory is not very common, either among sociologists or historians. I read an enormous amount of history and I depend on historians probably more than I do on sociologists, but I tend to assume that I will provide much of the theory. There are fashions in both disciplines, a period for example when a large amount of work is done on classes ("social history"), suddenly switching to great focus on ethnicity and nationalism, and class is forgotten. The connections between the two are neglected. There is a sociology of the military, but most of it is unconnected to the development of capitalism or the nation-state. The exceptional group here would be the economic historians who (unlike most economists) marry general economic theories to an appreciation of the development of real economic institutions.

General sociological theory relies on making connections among macro-level institutions. That is what I do and it is why I consider my model to be quite original among contemporary scholars, even though I see myself as sitting squarely in the classical tradition of Marx, Weber, and others. Many have identified me as "Weberian," rooted in the tradition laid down by Max Weber. Though I have numerous disagreements with Weber, I suppose there is some truth in that. But I do it my way.

References

Alesina, Alberto, & Edward L. Glaeser. 2004. *Fighting Poverty in the US and Europe: A World of Difference*. Oxford: Oxford University Press.

Chang, Ha-Joon. 2002. *Kicking Away the Ladder*. London: Anthem Press.

Dahl, Robert. 1989. *Democracy and Its Critics*. New Haven, Conn.: Yale University Press.

Eichengreen, Barry. 1996. *Globalizing Capital: A History of the International Monetary System*. Princeton, N.J.: Princeton University Press.

Fukayama, Francis. 1989. "The end of history?" *The National Interest*, Summer.

Gellner, Ernest. 1983. *Nations and Nationalism*. Ithaca, N.Y.: Cornell University Press.

Goldstone, Jack. 1991. *Revolution and Rebellion in the Early Modern World*. Berkeley: University of California Press.

Hall, John A. 2006. "Political questions." In J. A. Hall and R. Schroeder, eds., *An Anatomy of Power: The Social Theory of Michael Mann*. Cambridge, UK: Cambridge University Press.

Hall, John A. 2010. *Ernest Gellner: An Intellectual Biography*, London and New York: Verso.

Hirsch, Fred. 1976. *Social Limits to Growth*. Cambridge, Mass.: Harvard University Press.

Huntington, Samuel. 1991. *The Third Wave: Democratization in the Late Twentieth Century*. Norman: University of Oklahoma Press.

Jacobs, Margaret. 2000. "Commerce, industry and the laws of Newtonian science: Weber revisited and revised." *Canadian Journal of History*, 35.

Johnson, Chalmers. 2000. *Blowback: The Costs and Consequences of American Empire*. New York: Henry Holt.

Kohli, Atul. 2004. *State-Directed Development: Political Power and Industrialization in the Global Periphery*. Cambridge and New York: Cambridge University Press.

Laitin, David. 2006. "Mann's dark side: linking democracy and genocide." In J. A. Hall and R. Schroeder, eds., *An Anatomy of Power: The Social Theory of Michael Mann*. Cambridge, UK: Cambridge University Press.

Lipset, Seymour Martin. 1963. *Political Man*. London: Heinemann.

Mann, Michael. 2004. *The Dark Side of Democracy: Explaining Ethnic Cleansing*. Cambridge, UK: Cambridge University Press.

Mann, Michael. 1998. "The decline of Great Britain." In M. Mann, *States, War and Capitalism*. Oxford: Basil Blackwell.

Mann, Michael. 2004. *Fascists*. Cambridge, UK: Cambridge University Press.

Mann, Michael. 2003. *Incoherent Empire*. London and New York: Verso.

Mann, Michael. 1986. *The Sources of Social Power. Volume I: A History of Power from the Beginning to 1760 AD*. Cambridge, UK: Cambridge University Press.

Mann, Michael. 1993. *The Sources of Social Power. Volume II: The Rise of Classes and Nation-States, 1760–1914*. Cambridge, U.K.: Cambridge University Press.

Marshall, Thomas H. 1950. *Citizenship and Social Class, and Other Essays*. Cambridge, UK: Cambridge University Press.

Mills, C. Wright. 1959. *The Sociological Imagination*. New York: Oxford University Press.

Naughton, Barry. 1995. *Growing Out of the Plan: Chinese Economic Reform 1978–1993*. New York: Cambridge University Press.

Polanyi, Karl. 1957 [1944]. *The Great Transformation: The Political and Economic Origins of Our Time*. Boston: Beacon Press.

Schroeder, Ralph. 2007. *Rethinking Science, Technology, and Social Change*. Stanford, Calif.: Stanford University Press.

Senghaas, Dieter. 1985. *The European Experience: A Historical Critique of Development Theory*. Dover, N.H.: Berg Publishers.

Tilly, Charles. 1990. *Coercion, Capital, and European States, AD 990–1990*. Cambridge, Mass.: B. Blackwell.

Van Creveld, Martin. 2008. *The Changing Face of War*. New York: Ballantine Books.

Weiss, Linda, & John Hobson. 1995. *States and Economic Development: A Comparative Historical Analysis*. Cambridge, UK: Polity Press.